The Story of
Saint Sister Angelica

Jerry Walter

Dear Carol—
    I hope you enjoy reading this little book
as much as I enjoyed writing it.
                  Best wishes
                        Jerry Walter

ISBN 978-1-257-65263-1

Text and Cover Design: Anne Flanagan

Printing History:
First printing, 3 copies, privately published, July 1996
Second printing, open edition, Nighthawk Press, August 2011
Third printing, open edition, Nighthawk Press, May 2019

Author's Notes

This is a short story covering the life and times of a mythical Saint. The contents of the story were developed entirely within the imagination of the author. However, the historical figures and events are accurate within the limit of the author's research.

The story evolves from excerpts of the Saint's personal diary which has been translated from the French. The diary was preserved by the Saint's sister Emily and was discovered in Meaux, France, in 1610. The story also includes appropriate epilogues which were discovered at the same time, as well as a contemporary epilogue. It should be noted that the first several years of the diary were written by the Saint's sister Emily who was to have a great influence on her life.

The Cathedral of Notre Dame no longer exists as Saint Sister Angelica knew it. With dedicated work it will rise again from the ashes.

This story is dedicated to

Eulogio and Zoraida Ortega

Velarde, New Mexico
who are bringing the Holy Family and the Saints
into the homes and hearts of many,
through the creation of their santos.

Addendum to the dedication, April 2019. Eulogio Ortega (1917—2017) and Zoraida Ortega (1918—2012) are no longer with us and have gone to their final resting place. However, the religious art they created during their lifetimes will live on for decades to come.

Photograph of Eulogio and Zoraida Ortega, 1990, with a crucifix that they created.

Contents

Illustrations

Chapter 1
The Young Girl

1513

May 8, 1513.   It is my fifth birthday. All the fruit trees in Paris are covered with pink and white blossoms, and the warm air is so sweet. Mama and Papa had a grand party for me, with all the family singing happy melodies. The big surprise was that my brother Michael was here in his splendid uniform, having just returned with the army from Italy. Emily tied a big pink silk bow in my hair, and I looked so pretty in the mirror.

1515

July 12, 1515.   It is our favorite time of year, and once again we will travel to Meaux to spend a week with Grandmama and Grandpapa. It is a journey that takes a whole day along the dusty road. The road follows the Marne River which is lined with huge poplar trees. The wagon is piled high with luggage and gifts and provisions from the city.

July 14, 1515. How I love running in the yard with the geese and chickens and playing with the dogs. Grandmama fixes my favorite meals, but what I like most is the fresh warm bread with currant jelly. We all sleep together in a snug room in the thatched-roofed cottage. Just a short distance from the cottage is a tiny chapel that Grandpapa built many years ago. During our visit we spend an hour each day there. Some of the time is in silent meditation which I don't like very much because it is hard for me to keep still, but during the other times Grandpapa reads and tells stories about Jesus and priests and sisters and holy people. I like that the best.

July 17, 1515. It rained all day, and we all got very wet running back from the chapel. But soon Grandmama had steeped up a big pot of hot tea, which we drank very quickly.

July 20, 1515. We are all very sad because our week is up and it is time to return to Paris. A year is so very, very long to wait to return here. Before we left I visited the chapel once again by myself, and the sun was streaming in through the small round stained glass window with circular designs. How I love to stare at that window and feel the warm colors flow into me.

July 21, 1515. We got up before sunrise, had a quick breakfast, and boarded a flat boat which glided us back on the Marne River to Paris. It was so dark in the morning we could hardly see Grandmama and Grandpapa waving good-bye to us.

1516

February 19, 1516. Today I visited again with Papa at his apothecary shop. Whenever I visit he tells me much about all the powders and chemicals and syrups in the cloudy blue bottles. His partner Juan always looks so serious and I don't know if I like him very much. Papa and I took our lunch and walked over to the great Cathedral of Notre Dame. It is such a treat and makes my day with Papa even more interesting. Today I tried to count the number of great stone arches along the Cathedral walls, but I'm not very good with numbers yet. Emily is still teaching me. She is so smart.

Perhaps next year I will do better. During our walk we heard a merry tune in the air, and then spotted an organ grinder along the street with his little monkey. How much fun the little animal was, and Papa and I laughed as the organ grinder played his jolly melody and the monkey held out his little hat and danced about. But we are very sad about all the orphans in the streets, especially the little girls with their tattered clothes and hungry faces. I am so happy. I have Papa and Mama to love me. Papa gave one of the orphan girls a few coins.

July 17, 1516. We have returned again from the country and Grandmama and Grandpapa's farm. The dogs were so happy to see me. Grandmama taught me several new prayers in the chapel, which I have memorized by repeating them over and over. She gave me an extra-big hug when we departed early this morning. Grandpapa told the story of the round window in the chapel and how it came to be there. It was made by a glassworker who stayed at the farm for several months while working on windows for the Meaux Cathedral, and Grandpapa and Grandmama received it as a gift. The background is made of honey-colored glass that sparkles in the direct sunlight, and seems to fill me with a special message.

July 30, 1516. Michael is with us for a little while. I feel so full of life when he is around. He is having such great adventures in the service of King Francis. The favorite tale he tells happened early this spring. At the end of the stay of King Francis in Italy—in romantic sounding places like Rome and Milano—Michael was chosen to be one of the guards of the retinue which included the King and an artist named Leonardo da Vinci. The artist is quite old, Michael says, and the group traveled slowly through southern France, gradually winding their way north through the Loire Valley. Michael had the great opportunity to attend to the King and his artist guest at the great Chateau Fontainebleau. Then they traveled to Amboise where the artist is now living. It seems that Michael sometimes lives in a fairy tale, and when he tells the stories I travel along with him in my mind. I dream that some day I will be able to travel to some of these wonderful places, and Michael will be by my side.

September 8, 1516.　Papa has been telling of his learning when he was younger at the University of Paris, and the first books that he saw nearly 40 years ago. With the few coins that he earned he was able to purchase several of them. One of his best friends is Monsieur Henri Estienne; Papa met his father at the University during his schooling days. Monsieur Estienne is head of the Printers Guild, and on Tuesday Papa and I visited with him in the huge printing shop. The smell of the new books was so strong. Papa found several more books to add to his collection. Oh, how I want to be able to read all of them!

December 25, 1516.　We are all together this Christmas. Papa gave Mama a bright red scarf, all shiny like silk. Michael helped us all bundle up so we could visit the Cathedral to hear the Archbishop say Mass. It was so beautiful, with all the candles and the choir. I felt something inside of me that I hadn't felt before—a sense of closeness to Baby Jesus that seemed so real. After Mass we had great fun playing in the new snow.

1517

March 23, 1517.   I continue with my reading nearly every day. And Emily has shown me so much about writing this spring. Papa brings home any extra paper he has from the apothecary shop for me to write on. Michael has been gone again for two months. We never know where he is going and we just have to await his return to hear of his adventures.

July 14, 1517.   We have been in the country with Grandmama and Grandpapa for three days. The gardens are so fresh, and Grandpapa added some new color to the walls of the chapel. I so love sitting there in the chapel. Papa is not feeling well this time and is not his usual happy self. I pray that he will get better soon.

July 17, 1517.   We must leave a day early, for Papa is very ill. Grandmama gives me a special hug, and kisses me on the cheek. I always like to look in her eyes and see the kindness inside.

August 9, 1517.   Oh, this is the saddest of days, and Emily and Mama and I cried all day. Papa has died. Juan thinks it may have been caused by the chemicals. Papa had been sick for one month, and his skin had turned a horrible murky yellow color. We are all so sad and don't know what we will do. Michael is here to try to comfort us all.

August 11, 1517.   Papa was buried today. The sky was gray and the air was hazy. The common grave is just outside the city. Juan says that the shop is now his, and he will have a difficult time paying off the debts. He cannot promise Mama anything. Michael has a small amount of money and will try to help. Emily is already fifteen years of age and thinks she can learn to sew.

1518

January 1, 1518. Somehow we have made it to the new year. It has been a warm winter and we haven't needed to buy much wood. Emily is still teaching me all she knows from the books. Michael is off again in the service of King Francis.

May 8, 1518. This was not a happy birthday. Emily and I tried all day to cheer Mama up. She works very hard making soups and bread for the local vendor who peddles the foods along the street. Sometimes I don't think she is well.

July 1, 1518. We have decided that we cannot go to the country this year to visit with Grandmama and Grandpapa. There is no money, and the wagon fare is too expensive. Will I ever again see Grandmama's bright eyes, or hear Grandpapa's holy stories? Will I ever see the chapel again and feel the love of Jesus within it?

December 4, 1518. It has been very cold and Mama is terribly sick. Emily tries to do her cooking but can't make as much bread as Mama did, and so our money gets less and less.

December 25, 1518. Mama is gone. We sat up all Christmas Eve and prayed with her. We had her bundled up with all of our blankets. During the month Juan tried many of his medicines, but nothing would work. Oh, what is to become of us? I think of poor little Jesus in the crib and wonder how his plight could have been any worse than mine is now.

December 27, 1518. Only three from our family are at Mama's burial—Emily, I, and Mama's sister Suzanne. Grandmama and Grandpapa are too old to travel; Michael is in Italy. It will be several weeks, or even months, before they know of Mama's death. Emily looks so frail because she works so hard.

December 28, 1518. We have decided there is no way for us to stay together. Emily is old enough to share a room with her good friend Larrea. I am to go live with Aunt

Suzanne. How I will miss our family nest—the kitchen where we had the parties, the sitting room where Papa told stories and we prayed, and the cozy room where we all slept. It is time to pray for a brighter tomorrow.

1519

March 15, 1519.   Mama had never talked very much about Aunt Suzanne. She lives alone, but has several men friends. I have a little room of my own, and Aunt Suzanne treats me nicely and feeds me well. But she does not pray. I don't know why. I see Emily once a month on Sunday during and after Mass. She lives on the other side of the city and it is too far for either of us to travel very often. She gives me little books to read on all subjects. She said she tried to find Juan and the apothecary shop but it is gone.

October 3, 1519.   Emily visited today. She had very sad news. She had learned that both Grandmama and Grandpapa had died during the summer, one in May and the other in July. To me I always thought that death would escape them, for they seemed like such a permanent part of the farm and the landscape. Emily said I should meet her for special prayers at the Cathedral on Sunday.

1520

February 9, 1520.   It has been a good year with Aunt Suzanne. She laughs a lot and it is a happy place. Once in a while a man visits and they sing songs together. But after that I am glad I have my own room and little books to read.

Chapter 2
The Calling

April 25, 1520.   I have made a very special friend, and her name is April. She is thirteen, just a year older than I. April does not have a family and lives in a shelter with several other girls and an old caretaker. They seldom have enough to eat and I am able to share some of my meals with her. But Aunt Suzanne will not allow her to stay with me.

June 19, 1520.   April and I visited the Cathedral of Notre Dame today and spoke with a sister whose name is Sister Agatha. Sister Agatha is a very kind person and spent some time telling us legends about the building of the Cathedral. She told of the very holy people who have visited there, including Pope Pius II in the year 1461. She said we could come back any time, and I am sure we will.

September 2, 1520.   April has become very interested in my few books, and we are learning together. Emily shares books and papers with us whenever she can.

December 15, 1520.   A man and his son have come to live with Aunt Suzanne. The man's name is Hugh and the son's name is Robert. Hugh is a very stern man, and not like the happy and singing men that have visited with Aunt Suzanne in the past. Robert is a little older than I. This little place is very crowded with all of them here, and I spend more time with April. I do not like to be in the streets when it is cold, but April is very special to me and makes my troubles go away.

December 28, 1520.   This has not been a very good time. We did not have much of a Christmas celebration, and we did not attend Mass together. April and I talk about this and think it is very strange.

1521

February 4, 1521.   Aunt Suzanne and Hugh seem to have unusual ideas about the Church, and say mean things about the clergy. I do not believe what they say. Sometimes they are gone all day and they say they go to meetings about their own church ideas. I do not understand what is going on.

February 21, 1521.   Aunt Suzanne has forbidden me to pray or to attend Mass at the local parish or at the Cathedral. She says that my prayers are wrong, and I am under bad influence by the Church. I am very sad. When I pray my head is full of pleasant and holy thoughts, but Aunt Suzanne does not know what is secret in my mind.

February 27, 1521.   I say that I have arranged to meet Emily, but actually April and I sneak off to the Cathedral. We discuss the new situation about Aunt Suzanne and Hugh with Sister Agatha. Sister Agatha says that there are some new unbelievers in Paris who are following the forbidden writings of a heretic. I am very scared of what might happen, as there have been soldiers in and about the Churches trying to keep people from protesting. Sister Agatha says that I should do whatever Aunt Suzanne says.

March 30, 1521. I have been living in my own little world, and the rest of the people in the house have been living in theirs. I continue to pray in my own way and not say anything that will anger Aunt Suzanne or Hugh. Robert sees that I am sad and alone and tries to cheer me up sometimes. Once in a while he joins April and me in our visits around the neighborhood and to April's shelter. We all like being together. He has not yet met my sister Emily nor my brother Michael.

May 23, 1521. When we awoke this morning, Aunt Suzanne and Hugh were gone. We heard no noises during the night, but all signs of them have vanished. We know nothing of their friends, so do not know who to contact.

May 25, 1521. Oh, what are Robert and I to do, abandoned in these rooms? We have eaten nearly all the food. We are very scared. April is with us today, and we have sent a message to Emily.

May 30, 1521. April, Robert and I went to the Cathedral to consult with Sister Agatha. She says that some of the Lutherans, as she called them, have fled Paris for fear of their lives. She did not know any names. She secretly showed us a printed pamphlet, the likes of many she said have been distributed in the city. She said she did not know what it said, so we helped her read it. She became very disturbed, and asked us to leave and be careful. She said she must return to the nunnery to burn the printed words.

May 31, 1521. All three of us searched Aunt Suzanne's rooms carefully and found several of the printed pamphlets that so agitated Sister Agatha. They were beneath the shelves in the pantry. We read them completely first, and then burned them. We are fearful as to what they really mean. They take issue with the practices of Pope Leo. I did not know there was any struggle in the Church.

June 6, 1521. A messenger arrived this morning and we were very fearful of answering the door. But he assured us he had only important papers from Aunt Suzanne and Hugh, so we let him in. The package contained a long letter explaining their sudden departure. The fled quickly to Basel, Switzerland, and were now in Zurich with Hugh's brother. They did not know when they could return. They did not give the reason for their flight, but we knew. They said they were very sorry they had to abandon us, but hoped we could manage on our own. Also included in the package was a small amount of money. We were happy for that, as the landlord was by yesterday inquiring of their whereabouts.

July 8, 1521. There has been no further message from Aunt Suzanne and Hugh. We are very concerned about our well-being. The landlord says we must leave these rooms by Saturday if we have no more money.

July 21, 1521. We must move. For over two years I have lived in these rooms, since the death of Mama, and I think I have become a young woman with adult thoughts, because I am now thirteen. Emily thinks it will be okay for me to live with her and Larrea for a while. But I shall very much miss April and Robert. Robert has decided to become a laborer in the fields. April will again go to the shelter.

September 30, 1521. In spite of the love I find between Emily and me, I can no longer live in this place with Larrea. She has a terrible temper, and said she never wanted me here in the first place. Tomorrow I will visit the Cathedral and talk with Sister Agatha.

October 1, 1521. Sister Agatha and I talked for a very long time. In my loneliness I went into the Cathedral to pray by myself. As I sat there dwelling on the images of the saints, I sensed a great feeling inside my body. A flush swept over me, as though there was a presence surrounding me. A beam of sunlight flashed through the Cathedral. In the glow there was a message. It was my calling. I retreated to the nunnery and sought out Sister Agatha. We prayed together. I told her of my vision. I must enter the Convent. We quietly embraced. My course is set.

Chapter 3
The Convent

For the next eighteen months, there is no entry in Anne's diary. During this time she was in the Convent of Our Mother of Good Counsel, at L'Isle Adam, on the Oise River, just north of Paris, dedicated only to prayer and learning. No private writings were allowed.

1523

March 31, 1523. This is a blessed day. The Bishop of Saint Denis has said Mass with us, on this the day of completion of our studies. After Mass we repeated our Vows. I am to be called Sister Anne. Emily and Sister Agatha have been with me all day. How wonderful to see them after all these months. We cried together in joy. Emily said that Michael would visit when he returned to Paris. I am one of the younger women who is in this group. But I have discovered that I am quite different from the others, for I can read and write. And once again I can make entries in my diary. I am forbidden to write anything of what happened during the course of our studies for the past eighteen months.

May 8, 1523.   I am now fifteen, and will be staying at the Convent for three more years, dedicated to prayer and assisting with the care of the house and gardens. I have found a great friend in Mother Superior, who is sharing with me the wisdom of her years here at the Convent.

July 11, 1523.   I have sent a message to Emily to send some of the books. I think we are in desperate need of a library here at the Convent. Some of the sisters would prefer not to read, and are satisfied with cooking, gardening, embroidery work, and praying. Others would care to read only special prayers, stories about the lives of the saints, and words of meditation. But there are several who feel a need to learn of the great world around them.

September 7, 1523.   At last I have seen Michael again. What a splendid brother he is! What a gallant soldier! He spoke again of his adventures. I could not contain myself, nor he himself. I quickly gathered several of the sisters and had him repeat his stories. He spoke of the great art treasures he had seen in Italy. In Milano he saw a huge fresco by Leonardo da Vinci entitled "Last Supper." He described the vibrant colors—the strong lavenders and browns of the background scene, the delicate color of the skin, the bright reds, greens, blues and golds of the robes and the careful white and gray shadowing in the table cover. Michael told of the precise placement of the thirteen figures, and the look of pious sorrow on the face of Jesus. He also informed us that this great Italian artist had died four years earlier in Amboise, much to the sorrow of King Francis. Michael spoke of Rome! Oh, would that I could visit there—to accompany him on his next expedition with King Francis! Michael described the soaring ceiling in the Sistine Chapel and the hundreds of sacred luminous figures. The art in the Chapel was completed only three years earlier by an artist called Michel Angelo. What wonders there must be to behold in this place! The other sisters were aglow with hearing of such great religious art. I could sense their excitement upon hearing of the depiction of spirituality and the glory of God that flowed from the brushes of these great Italian artists.

December 12, 1523. The time is passing slowly here. I feel there is more that I must do. I have sent a messenger to Monsieur Estienne bearing a letter describing the deplorable lack of learning materials at the Convent. Could he spare a selection of books? Could he pay a call to tell of the latest publications?

December 25, 1523. On this day, as on all Christmas Days, the sisters of this Convent repeat their Vows, with dedication to Our Holy Mother, the Mother of Good Counsel. It is beautiful to be here. It is beautiful to be enveloped in the radiance of the love we all share.

1524

January 9, 1524. My silent prayers have been answered. Today arrived a carriage containing six boxes of new books from the Estienne Publishing House. But to my surprise, Mother Superior was very skeptical. Had I done something wrong? She must consult with the Bishop first. What could there be wrong with books? With writing? With knowledge? With truth?

January 10, 1524. The Bishop and his aides inspected the books very carefully. They asked if I was aware that heretical publications were being widely distributed throughout France, writings damaging to the Church and to France herself. I told them I was aware of such writings of several years ago, but I knew nothing of their abundance today. Finally, all of the books were passed by the Bishop, and placed in the library. Those sisters who sought contact with the outside world—the great new inventions, the political and social upheaval, and the tales of adventure in new lands—were astonished and excited; those who thought it our calling to look only inward were embarrassed by the enthusiasm. But we continued to live and grow in knowledge and prayer.

March 23, 1524. At last Monsieur Henri Estienne has paid a visit. He spoke to a group of us in the library. He told of the hundreds of secular books that were now being printed, and how we were on the threshold of the golden age of personal writing and publishing. He is personally assisting King Francis in establishing the Royal Library in Paris. In addition, the Newsbook Guild quickly—in a matter of only months—could bring the latest happenings in all of Europe together in current periodicals, available to all who could read. He then addressed the issue of religious writing, and how the Roman Catholic theologians at the Sorbonne kept a watchful eye on all religious documents available in Paris. Anxious to please the local Archbishop, he personally previewed all publications sent for printing. It was an inspiring day, and we all wished for his speedy return.

1525

January 18, 1525. Last year was a fine year at the Convent. Even those sisters who looked only inward found use of the library. The Convent has been known for producing exceptional religious embroidery for vestments for Mass, and for other uses on altars and in the sanctuaries. One of the books that arrived in November detailed new techniques and patterns recently developed in Brugge in the Duchy of Flanders. The innovative sisters quickly adopted the new techniques, and by mid-January displayed sparkling new design elements in their work. One, created by Sister Marlene, had intricate crosses intertwined with hearts and vines, and we all marveled at the pattern and details.

April 1, 1525. The beginning of this month always reminds me of my friend April. Emily has visited the Convent several times the past year, and in spite of searching in the housing area where Aunt Suzanne and I once lived, April could not be found. I worry and pray for her safety, and hope one day we can see one another again and talk about the courses of our lives.

April 9, 1525. Word has reached the Convent of the capture of King Francis in Pavia in Italy, and the great loss at the siege of Milano. My concern is with my dear brother Michael. Was he in the encampment? When shall I know?

July 12, 1525. Once again we have word of King Francis and that he is being held in Madrid by King Charles of Spain. The whereabouts of Michael is unknown. I pray every day for his safe return.

December 31, 1525. The year is completed without word from Michael. It is a sad year. Have I lost my brother? And my best friend April? My prayers to the Lord are full of entreaties.

1526

February 19, 1526. It has been a cold, dark winter. Hardly have we seen the sun. The chapel windows are ashen and lifeless, and not radiating the usual warmth that I feel when I am surrounded by them. The conversations in the sewing room are meaningless. I even feel dullness in the library, always my one source of strength save the chapel. I sit with Mother Superior in boredom and anguish. Where can I find hope? Strength once again? A sense of purpose? What can restore my mind? My heart? My sense of love? Oh, Lord, help me to find an answer!

April 19, 1526. King Francis is back in Paris! Word has reached us of his release and speedy travel over the Pyrenees to Bayonne, Bordeaux, and Fontainebleau.

April 25, 1526. It is a miracle! Michael appeared in the doorway today. No, not a vision, not a dream as I first thought. I ran to him. I touched him. It was Michael! We embraced. My prayers have been answered. We spent the entire day together. I spoke of my continual prayers. I spoke candidly of my lack of sense of purpose which had developed during my three years here at the Convent. I spoke of my continued love for my vocation and calling.

And Michael spoke of his year-long detainment, in the company of King Francis. He was selected to be one of the three Frenchmen to accompany and aid the King during his captivity, first in Italy and later in Barcelona and Madrid. He saw to the King during his severe illness—thought by the attending Spanish physicians as the King's deathbed. He saw the King's miraculous recovery in the presence of the King's sister Marguerite, as communion was about to be served during Mass in his prison chapel. Michael heard the King utter "It is my God who will cure my body and soul. I pray I may receive." The consecrated wafer was divided between Marguerite and her brother, and everyone in the room fell down by the King's bedside and gave thanks.

Michael also accompanied the King during his return to France, riding with him among the spring blossoms throughout the foothills and valleys of Aquitaine Basin. The apple and pear blossoms scented the air with life-renewing fragrance. The King was very grateful for Michael's continued loyalty.

April 26, 1526. Michael returned today, for we were not completed with our conversation of yesterday. After all, it had been well over two years since last we spoke! We continued to search through my anguish and discontent. We spoke of Mama and Papa, of Grandmama and Grandpapa, of Emily and April, of Sister Agatha, and Aunt Suzanne and Hugh and Robert. Michael wondered if I had recently spoken with Sister Agatha. I hadn't. "Could you leave the Convent for a day?" he asked.

"Let me consult with Mother Superior." We found her at the business desk, posting receipts for embroidery work. I spoke. I would very much like to visit with Sister Agatha. Michael would accompany me. May I leave the Convent for one day?"

Mother Superior's gaze fell past me to the elaborate stained glass window on the far wall depicting the Savior of Our Redemption. In quiet reflection she said, "Yes, Sister Anne, you may go. Sister Agatha was your mentor. You need once more to consult with her." Michael beamed, and so did I. She added, "Tomorrow should be a nice spring day for the trip." I fell down and put my head in Mother Superior's lap, and wept with joy and relief.

April 27, 1526. And it was a beautiful spring day. Michael pulled up to the Convent door in a hired carriage, just after breakfast prayers were over. The other sisters wished me a good day, and off we went. It had been so long! The fresh breeze smacked my cheeks, and my veil nearly blew off! Memories swarmed over me. We drove past the rooms where last I saw Aunt Suzanne. We trotted through the neighborhood where last I saw April and Robert. And we could still both identify the location of the apothecary shop, where Papa earned his living and provided so well for us. At last we rounded the corner by the Cathedral. We passed through the gates to the nunnery. And there, inside, was Sister Agatha, smiling broadly as she identified me scurrying toward her. We hugged, all three of us, for she had heard of Michael's loyal service to the King.

Sister Agatha read my eyes. "You're looking for counsel. It has been three years. Let us talk." Michael joined us as we sat in the study. We reviewed the earlier years.

"What would really please you, Sister Anne?" she asked. "How would you really like to expand your calling?"

"I think mostly of April, and all the other little orphan girls I've seen in the streets over the years. Is there some way I could help them?"

"You are young, and very ambitious. There is great need for assistance in this area. Orphanages to give girls protective care are very few, and volunteer labor is practically nonexistent. Just recently I spoke with a Bishop about this and he is anxious to tackle the problem."

"What Bishop was that, may I ask?"

"Bishop Briçonnet, of Meaux. Do you know where that is?"

Both Michael and I called out at once. "Meaux!" "Meaux!"

"Meaux, that is the town of Grandmama and Grandpapa," I explained. "It has been eight years since we last visited the farm. Both Grandmama and Grandpapa are gone, we know. What would have happened to the farm land? And the buildings?"

"Only the Town Office Clerk would know," said Michael. "I could go to Meaux to find out later this week. And maybe at the same time I could visit with the Bishop to inquire of his orphanage plans. Could I get a letter with your seal, Sister Agatha?"

"Certainly, Michael. But first, let us visit the Cathedral and pray together for inspiration and guidance."

Michael and I returned to the Convent just before dinner prayers. Mother Superior was delighted to hear how we spent the day.

May 3, 1526.   My life has been filled with anticipation since Michael departed just one week ago. Mother Superior even heard me singing in the Abbey. The grayness has left, and I feel illumination all around me—during my tasks and conversations, and especially during my prayers.

May 5, 1526.   Michael returned. He had a mischievous sparkle in his eyes. "What's going on, Michael?" I started.

"Something just in time for your birthday," he replied. I had actually forgotten my birthday was only three days away. "Let's find Mother Superior and discuss this together."

"I just returned from Meaux," he began. Mother Superior took sharp notice. "First I visited the Town Office Clerk. Seven years ago, when Grandmama and Grandpapa died, no one came forward to claim the farm and tend to its care. So the property came under the care of the Town Land Steward. The buildings are very run down, but the land remains cultivated by tenant farmers. If legal heirs were to appear, they could claim the land as their own."

"We are the legal heirs, aren't we Michael? You and Emily and I?"

"Yes, we are Anne. Yes, we are! But let me continue. I spent some time with Bishop Briçonnet and his staff. The Bishop is definitely interested in starting an orphanage. He would be willing to support it financially, for the first few years at least, until it got started. He thinks a perfect place would be the old farm, if we would agree."

"Oh, Michael, let's do it. Let's do it now," I gushed, but then paused. "I wonder how Emily would feel about this?"

"I've already taken care of that," said Michael. "I saw her yesterday, and she is totally in favor of the project."

"Do I have a say in this?" We had nearly forgotten that Mother Superior was in the room. "Don't forget, Sister Anne, that you are still under my absolute care until you are twenty years of age."

"But that's two years away!" I exclaimed.

"If you are really sure of yourself, Sister Anne, and I think you are, I will not stand in your way."

And so was born the Meaux Orphanage for Girls.

Chapter 4
The Orphanage

June 9, 1526.　The last month has been busy with preparation, and Michael and I have been working very closely together. He has made three trips to Meaux and the farm. Bishop Briçonnet has lent two laborers from his staff to help repair the buildings. Michael says there is so very much work to do. But I am so willing. The sense of anticipation has me so excited inside. And I do think some of this anticipation has rubbed off on several of the other sisters.

June 12, 1526.　Today was my last day at the Convent. I spent much time with Mother Superior, seeking her guidance, and we prayed together in the chapel. I realize how much strength I need to depart on this unknown mission. I sought this strength today by gathering my best friends—the sisters—together in the chapel after noon prayers, where we sang and prayed aloud. This has buoyed me up; I hope the strength will last. I am frightened of the unknown.

June 14, 1526.   I was far too tired yesterday to write in my journal. Michael arrived at dawn at the Convent with a huge horse-drawn cart. We piled all my meager belongings into the cart, as well as provisions that have been donated by Mother Superior and the sisters. They bade us a warm farewell and we were off down the dirt road to Meaux. Even though it was only thirty-five miles from the Convent at L'Isle Adam to Meaux, the country roads were terrible, not yet repaired from the spring rains. At dusk we stopped at the roadside shelter at Juilly; Michael stayed up most of the night protecting our cart from thieves. We finally arrived here at the farm at noon.

The farm is in far worse condition than I expected. One of the walls of the cottage has collapsed, the roof is in complete need of replacement, and most of the tables and stools have disappeared. The stables and coops are barely useable. But the chapel is intact! Grandpapa must have repaired the walls and roof just before he died. How delightful it was to stand inside its walls again, to feel its comfort and peace, and to be in the presence of my favorite circular window of light. But I could stay only for a moment, for there is much work to do.

June 21, 1526.   This has been the most difficult week of my life. How weary we are from the work. We have made friends with several nearby tenant farmers, and a large adjacent farm is occupied by a free farmer who owns his land. They are very happy about the restoration work we are doing, and are so proud that soon there will be an orphanage within the buildings.

June 22, 1526.   It is Sunday, and for the first time I met Bishop Briçonnet after Mass at the Meaux Cathedral. He looked quite austere, but after we talked for a while we took a liking to one another. He too is proud of the goals we have set. We spoke of the assistance he promised to give, and we laid out our needs. Our biggest need was for seed, and assistance in planting crops to carry us through the winter.

It is already late June, and everything must be planted within the week. He gave his full support.

July 2, 1526.   The crops are in. Only with the Bishop's assistance, and the support of the neighbors, could we have reclaimed this land so quickly, brought it under cultivation, and restored the vineyards. Together we ended every day in the chapel, giving thanks for the favors the Lord has bestowed on us.

August 4, 1526.   The garden vegetables and grain are flourishing. Chickens and geese are once again scurrying about the yard. Some fruit is ripening on the old trees, but they are in much need of pruning next year. With the help of neighbors this is a wonderful summer. Soon we will be able to bring out the first orphan girls.

August 14, 1526.   Our blessings have been many. But Michael must leave. He received word that once again King Francis needs his personal services for political business in Paris. Whatever shall I do without him? But Michael must remain loyal to the King.

August 17, 1526.   Oh, what a happy, happy day. Michael and I attended Mass today at the Meaux Cathedral, to pray for his quick return, for he must leave tomorrow. As we walked past the Sunday fruit stands in the Cathedral courtyard, I spied a face in the shaded stall that I thought look familiar. Could it be? Yes, it was! It was April! My long lost friend April! We hugged in sheer joy. It has been nearly five years since we said good-bye in the streets of Paris. We had so much to tell, and we chatted on so loudly and gleefully that everyone thought we were two little girls who had lost their senses.

Her story quickly told: April had left the shelter and followed Robert who chose to become a laborer in the fields. They wandered from farm to farm along the Marne

River, and finally located here near Meaux. April and Robert have married and have a son, Gregory. April is so very happy, and so delighted that I have come back into her life. Tomorrow she will bring Robert and the little boy to the farm. And oh how I need her friendship beginning once again on the very day that Michael is leaving.

August 18, 1526.   Robert, April and Gregory arrived just as Michael was leaving. Oh how wonderful to see Robert again. And Gregory has April's precious smile. What tears I shed on Michael's departure. How much emotion can be experienced in one day? Robert and April have promised as much help as they can give to the Orphanage.

September 30, 1526.   The first two orphan girls have arrived. They are little dears, only six and eight, who have been selected by Sister Agatha, and have been transported here personally by Emily. We are just barely ready. The cottage has been made weather tight, for the winter could be early. Bishop Briçonnet has provided funds for the materials needed. Robert has been very helpful in planning the work. He himself became an orphan, for he has never heard again from his father Hugh. This is Emily's first visit since we began the restoration, and together in the chapel we shared memories of the past. As we sat on the makeshift bench, the sun was beaming through my favorite round window and shedding warmth on this new reunion.

October 18, 1526.   The crops have all been harvested. The cold cellar is full. There have been donations of food from the neighbors.

December 25, 1526.   We had a long Christmas prayer in the chapel. Robert built a little fire in a temporary stove, and it was warm and cozy. Several of the neighbors came in with greetings, and we lit candles together. Our two orphan girls took such delight in the new family they have found.

1527

February 10, 1527.   A message was received today from Bishop Briçonnet that three more orphan girls are in urgent need of shelter. Can Sister Agatha send them up? I conferred with the other girls. Are they willing to share their little food and space? They both said, "Yes, Jesus will provide. Sister Anne, we are so grateful for your sharing this cottage with us. Let us in turn share it with others."

February 26, 1527.   Emily has brought the three new orphan girls to the farm. It was a cold, blustery day, and all seven of us huddled by the fire and shared hot chicken broth and bread. Emily and I whispered far into the night, after the girls were sound asleep, as to Emily's future. "Could I plan to come share the burdens of the Orphanage in the summer?" she asked. "Would you let me help administer the tasks and tend to the girls? After all, this is your project, and I wouldn't want to interfere or intrude."

"Oh, Emily, you are my very own sister," I replied. "This farm, this land, are both of ours, and Michael's, too. We have endured so much together. Please plan to come for good as soon as you are able." From that moment we sensed a bond new to both of us.

April 20, 1527.   Robert and April spent the day and we talked of plans for the Orphanage. Robert has spent much time working out details of expansion. "Expansion!" I declared. "But we've only barely started to provide a few basic needs. Isn't it too early?"

I shouldn't ever be a doubter, I sensed, with Robert around. He said he can make it happen, with April, and Emily after she arrives. "If you will have us, April and I have decided to dedicate ourselves to this wonderful Orphanage. First we must get the garden planted, and the fields sown," said Robert. "I think we can start tomorrow. Let us all trust in our faith in God."

An old etching of the Nativity

I retreated to the chapel to find comfort, and renew my trust that we were performing the Lord's Will.

May 8, 1527. Emily has arrived, bringing two more girls. Now we have seven. I pray every day that we can give them the protection they need, and provide for their future. There is so much to do, so much to do. It was a wonderful birthday. Emily gave me a gift of wonder and surprise. Many years ago Papa gave Mama a red silk scarf for Christmas, which Emily kept after Mama's death. Today she presented it to me. We decide that it will make a perfect addition to the chapel, for it contains a pattern of small blue crosses on its background of red.

August 29, 1527. The summer has passed quickly, and with a lot of commotion at the Orphanage. We now have ten girls. Robert has laid out the plans for a new dormitory building near the old cottage to house the girls. There will also be a large room for instructions. During the summer Emily and I developed a complete course of learning for the girls. Our foundation is the small library that Emily kept, starting with Papa's books, and also those she collected herself, purchased with her sewing money.

September 15, 1527. Today we broke ground for the dormitory. April created a wonderful meal for all those involved, from the fruits and vegetables of the season. She is so terribly efficient in the kitchen.

November 3, 1527. Robert and the neighbors worked hard on the dormitory foundations, and have the timbers laid up, ready for the first walls. They plan to work on the structure all winter, so it will be ready for spring.

December 25, 1527. Once again we had a large Christmas celebration. Emily and I worked most of the month preparing for the activities. The girls were astonished. The chapel was festive, with candles all about. During the lighting of the candles a thought flashed through my mind of the Mass at Notre Dame Cathedral and all the glory that was present there so many years ago. I felt once again my closeness with Baby Jesus. Then, magically, a surprise greeted us. A local wood craftsman, Eulogio, delighted us by bringing in a carving of the Baby Jesus. He carried it devoutly in his arms. Robert spontaneously fashioned a small crib, and tears welled up in my eyes and all the girls' eyes when the little statue was placed on the bed of straw. We all sang Christmas songs of love and joy, and for me a special remembrance.

1528

February 24, 1528.   The dormitory is quickly rising, and it will be beautiful. All the girls are excited about having a home of their own. We were very honored today to have Bishop Briçonnet pay us a personal visit. He was amazed at the progress that has been made, and we thanked him for his great assistance. Later, he gave us all his special blessing in the chapel.

June 18, 1528.   At last the dormitory is finished. So many people have helped this spring, taking time out from their hard labor in the fields. The wood craftsman Eulogio has fashioned simple beds for each of the girls. The books have been moved onto shelves attached to a special wall in the instruction room. There are not enough tables and chairs, but all that will come, we pray.

June 28 1528.   We have received a special message from the Convent. Oh, has it been over two years since I left? So very much has happened since then. Mother Superior informs me that word of the great progress at the Orphanage has spread, and several sisters at the Convent are interested in relocating. "Sister Anne, could you use their assistance?" she asked. "I have two special sisters in mind—Sister Zoraida and Sister Johnetta. I'm sure you remember them. Sister Zoraida is skilled in weaving and artistic painting, and Sister Johnetta has developed her talent in music. They sincerely would like to join you." I replied immediately that I would lovingly await their arrival.

August 5, 1528.   Sister Zoraida and Sister Johnetta are here and have swept us up in their enthusiasm. They have virtually taken over all the instruction of the girls. In addition, Sister Johnetta has introduced us to the inspiring choral music of Josquin des Prés. They also brought two more girls with them when they arrived three weeks ago. With April tending to most of the kitchen chores, Robert tending to the buildings and fields, and Emily assisting in the planning, my dreams for this Orphanage, through the divine assistance of God, are developing before my very eyes.

December 25, 1528.   What a marvelous Christmas celebration we had. But this year, I was the one who was to be totally surprised. Secretly the girls had been talking to Eulogio and Sister Zoraida. At noon today the girls, all giddy with excitement, blindfolded me and led me to the chapel. When they took the blindfold off, before me, high on the wall below the round stained glass window, was a nearly life-sized carved angel. Its robes flowed all around, the magnificent wings were outspread, and the hands carried a crucifix and a Bible. The colors were astonishing—the most beautiful of blue in the robes, the wings all in ivory, and the face painted with a glowing and serene expression. The girls had to hold me up for fear I might collapse. It was the most wonderful thing I had ever seen—an Angel in Blue. "Tell me," I asked, with a nearly fainting voice, "why—how—when did this all happen?"

"Woodcarver Eulogio carved the angel, and Sister Zoraida painted it. Isn't it beautiful? It's our special gift to you, Sister Anne," they all chimed in together. "You are more than Sister Anne to us. To us, you are an angel, our own personal angel. To us you are not Sister Anne, but Sister Angelica. Sister Angelica! Sister Angelica!" they chanted as they danced around me. And I sat down and hugged each one of them as tightly as if they were a part of my own being.

December 27, 1528. To add to the joys of this Christmas season, Michael has joined us again, and said that he can spend several months. I have spent much time today in grateful prayer for the gift of Michael, Emily and I being together again, and for my new and growing family here at the Orphanage.

1529

January 31, 1529. Upon a petition to the Convent of Our Mother of Good Counsel, my name has been changed to Sister Angelica. Mother Superior delighted in my tale of the Christmas Angel, and hopes to visit the Orphanage soon.

March 3, 1529. It has been a dreary winter, even with all the excitement in and about the Orphanage. Michael was here until two weeks ago. Even the girls are a little depressed with the gray sky. To cheer them, I composed a short poem which they all have memorized:

Thank You Lord:
For each new day you give to me,
For earth and sky and sand and sea;
For rainbows after springtime showers,
Autumn leaves and summer flowers;
For winter snowscapes so serene,
Harvest fields of gold and green;
For beauty shining all around;
Lilac scent and robin sound;
For stars that twinkle high above,
And all the people that I love.
Amen.

June 18, 1529. Robert and Eulogio are talking of plans to enlarge the chapel during the next year. This is a most exciting plan, and we have all taken turns in drawing a few ideas of our own. Bishop Briçonnet has given his blessing on the project, and artisans in his employ will give assistance.

August 3, 1529.　The major addition to the chapel has begun. The farmers from all around are all working with us, for we hope to have the Bishop consecrate this as a Church, so a neighborhood Mass can be held in it every Sunday.

August 8, 1529.　There came a word of caution from the Bishop. A requirement of the Church is that any consecrated Church must contain a sacred relic. The Bishop has none to contribute. Unless we can locate such an object, regular Masses cannot be said here. All of us in our expanded family—Emily, Robert, April, Sister Zoraida, Sister Johnetta, Eulogio, all nineteen girls, and even little Gregory, who is now six, are very disappointed. I spent much of the evening meditating in the old part of the chapel for guidance, praying that God's Will should again be done.

September 10, 1529.　Work has slowed on the chapel addition. There is much to harvest this year. The fruits, vegetables and grains are abundant. The grapes are nearly ready to pick. All of the girls are delighted to work in the fields during part of the day helping out. They see every day the gifts of God.

October 4, 1529.　I had been sitting in the chapel alone, meditating on the importance of all our work and thankful for the gifts that God has been giving to us. Suddenly, I was dazed by a glowing light seeming to come from the area of the red scarf with blue crosses which was hanging on the wall near the altar. The light pulsed several times, then disappeared. A few moments later the phenomenon repeated, and again disappeared. All was quiet. I approached the scarf, and sensed a warmth radiating from the wall. But there was nothing visible, and nothing was moving or disturbed. I returned to my seat, and contemplated the strange sensation. An inner voice told me there was one person I must confide in—Robert.

Robert and Gregory were in the garden. "Come with me, please, Robert." He was surprised by my shaking voice. We walked through the outside construction area of the church, and as we stood in the chapel I recalled my vision to him. "You must search for something, something behind the scarf, within the wall," I heard myself saying. "Something very important is here with us." Unable to speak any more in my faintness, Robert helped me to my study in the cottage. Emily tended to me, all curious about the commotion.

Several hours later I had just recovered my composure when Robert came running in all excited. "Look what we found!" he shouted, quite unlike Robert who always has full control of himself. "We removed a part of the rear wall that was discolored near the altar, and we discovered this metal box. What do you make of it, Sister Angelica?"

Carefully we opened the box, and inside was a small piece of brown cloth. Also, there was a small piece of brittle paper, like parchment, with a short inscription. "Can you read it, Sister Angelica?" asked Robert.

"I can read a few of the words, but not all," I replied. "The message is in Latin. Let us show it to Sister Johnetta who has studied Latin extensively through her music training."

Sister Johnetta was astonished at the find. She crossed herself. "This could be very significant. Yes, this is Latin. The message is very hard to make out, but the words seem to be: 'Cloth woven by Brother Joseph, F.O., for Francis Bernadone, 1220 A.D. Seal P.H. III 1230'."

"I do not know for certain what that means," continued Sister Johnetta, "although I can guess. Francis Bernadone was Saint Francis of Assisi. He died in 1228, October,

I believe. The Seal could be that of Pope Honorius III. I believe we should take this to Bishop Briçonnet."

October 8 1529. The metal box with the cloth was delivered to the Bishop today, together with a full explanation of the finding. He said he will present it to his scholars for their interpretation. We are all very excited at the Orphanage.

October 11, 1529. Bishop Briçonnet and two of his scholars arrived by carriage today, quite unannounced. Indeed, Sister Johnetta's speculations were true. The cloth was from the hood of Saint Francis of Assisi. The dates and weaving have been verified. The cloth is identical to that seen first-hand by Scholar Andrew during his duty tour with Elector Frederick the Wise at the Castle Church in Wittenberg, Saxony.

The Bishop asked to see the site of the findings, and we all gathered around the wall excavation. "What date did you discover this?" he asked.

"Just seven days ago," replied Robert.

"Then we have a sacred occurrence," responded the Bishop, "for October 4 is the feast of Saint Francis. This is a genuine religious relic." We all knelt at the spot, and the Bishop gave a special blessing. And he spoke of the Church, yes "Church", that was soon to be consecrated on this spot, the Church of Saint Francis of Assisi. This has been a very special day for the Orphanage.

December 25, 1529. This Christmas we all look forward to the completion of the Church next year. The celebration in the chapel was festive, for Emily and I created a special Procession of the Candles. The celebrants all filed into the chapel, which was in virtual darkness except for two candles near the Baby Jesus. Candles were then passed to everyone, and they each filed past the candles at the Crib and lighted their own candles. Soon, the entire chapel was awash in the soft golden glow of many flickering candles. What a wonderful sight to behold. The girls knew that Jesus in the Crib was pleased.

1530

February 9, 1530.   This has been a special winter for us. One of the neighbors brought in a great deal of wool from the sheep they have been raising, and Sister Zoraida and Emily have been teaching the girls how to spin and weave. We boiled some of the skins from the onions in the cold cellar and dyed some of the wool red; the carrots also gave a unique color. Sister Zoraida is very good at creating designs, and Emily showed off her sewing skills again. This has been a great project, and both Robert and Eulogio have been innovating new designs in the construction of the spinning wheels and looms.

March 19, 1530.   It is the feast of Saint Joseph, and in his memory a new invention has been given to the Orphanage. It is an iron plow. It is clean and shiny, and will be a welcome replacement for the wooden plow that Eulogio has had such a difficult time keeping in repair.

April 30, 1530.   Work on the church has continued all winter as best it could, but the weather has not cooperated. There has been much cold and snow. But now it is spring, and the daffodils are bobbing their yellow heads throughout the garden.

August 4, 1530.   Michael has returned to the Orphanage. Once again Michael had been on a special mission for King Francis. When the King was released from his detainment in Spain, he had to present his two sons, Henry and Charles, as hostages, who were to be held until certain conditions of the treaty were fulfilled. They have been held for over four years, but were finally released on July 2. Michael was placed in charge of their return to Paris, and what patriotic celebrations took place along the route of their homecoming. Michael also told of the gratitude the King expressed for the reunion. All of Paris is thankful the ordeal is over.

August 18, 1530.   Four of the most beautiful windows for the new Church have arrived from the Bishop's glass artisan in Meaux. They are all in stained glass and detail four scenes from the life of young Jesus: The Flight into Egypt, Sitting with the Teachers in the Temple, the Baptism by Saint John, and The Marriage Feast at Cana.

December 17, 1530.   This is our great day. The Church of Saint Francis of Assisi has been consecrated. The relic of the Hood of Saint Francis is encased in a special glass cabinet to the side of the altar for all to view. It was a beautiful ceremony, and sunlight was streaming in through the bright stained glass windows. The magnificent Angel in Blue was looking down on all of us, and even Bishop Briçonnet was astounded by its beauty and presence. Mother Superior and two other sisters from the Convent made the long journey to be with us on this blessed day. Many neighbors crowded into their new Church, and the rafters rang with sacred song, for Sister Johnetta had obtained copies of some wonderful new music from the English choirmaster of Cardinal College in Oxford named John Taverner. During the feast that followed, with lots of wonderful flatcakes that April had created especially for the day, Emily, Michael and I could only wonder what Grandpapa and Grandmama were thinking as they looked down on us, looked down on the beautiful Church that once was the family chapel.

December 25, 1530.   All of the neighbors and many folks from Meaux came to witness the Procession of the Candles. It was a beautiful day, and many material contributions were given to the Orphanage in honor of Baby Jesus.

1531

January 17, 1531.   Monsieur Henri Estienne arrived by carriage. He had been speaking with Mother Superior, and she told him of the work we were doing here. He brought with him a large collection of books, beautiful books, for the library. He was so enthused by what he saw that he did not leave until dark. "I'm the guest of Bishop Briçonnet for the evening. We must go over his new printing press needs. He has a small publishing room, you know. But I would like to return tomorrow. Perhaps there are areas in which I can be of assistance here."

January 18, 1531.   Monsieur Estienne returned by mid-morning. "Sister Angelica," he began, "you have educated yourself in the arts and letters, and have great interest in sharing this knowledge with others—all these girls, for instance." I didn't know what was coming next. "You have a small area in the instruction room that I would like to fill with a small printing press. It is old, and some of the type is worn, but it should suffice in getting you started."

I was shocked. A printing press in our Orphanage? Was it allowed? I knew of the many problems that the press had created throughout Europe. I knew of the repression that was being conducted by the Church for writings that were in conflict with the teachings. The press was responsible for wide dissemination of new ideas, not always consistent with the thinking of the Church.

"Bishop Briçonnet has endorsed this idea," he said, reading my mind. "This would be a great opportunity. Would you accept?"

I could hardly contain myself. "Of course! Progress and education and books right here in the Orphanage." It was so much more than I had ever imagined!

February 14, 1531.   Eulogio has been busy building trays for the type and shelves for the inking, per Monsieur Estienne's instructions. And the press arrived today.

What a strange sensation that we ourselves will be able to print stories and thoughts of our own for others to read. It will be a great challenge to keep to our other necessary tasks.

March 19, 1531.   Three more girls have arrived from Paris. We now have thirty-one here, and the dormitory is nearly at capacity. But with God's Will we shall grow, prosper and provide.

April 9, 1531.   It is Easter Sunday, and the Church was filled with neighbors and visitors. It is so wonderful having regular Sunday Mass right here at the Orphanage. Father Leonard comes faithfully every Sunday from Meaux out of the courtesy of Bishop Briçonnet.

May 30, 1531.   We have printed our first book. It is small, but a start. It is a speller and reader for the young girls, and the contents were written by Emily and me. We ended the book with a story I wrote about Saint Anne, mother of Mary, and an imaginary cat that belonged to Saint Anne. The girls were delighted when they read it. We printed and bound 50 copies during the past month. It is the first time we had any textbooks at the Orphanage.

September 17, 1531.   About 100 books have arrived, a gift from Monsieur Etienne. Included was a new dialogue relating to the founding of new lands to the west by an Italian explorer, Cristoforo Colombo. His travels and explorations had been sponsored by Queen Isabella of Castile and King Ferdinand of Aragon. Another revealing book in the group is by Niklas Kopernik, an astronomer from Poland, who speaks of his theory of the earth revolving on its axis and moving around the sun. Scholars are startled by this new theory. It is impossible for me to comprehend.

December 25, 1531.   This Christmas Emily and I surprised all the girls with a gift from the printing press. We had created a special booklet with writings about

Christmas and the Holy Birth. Sister Zoraida drew some special illustrations on wood, Eulogio carved out the designs in the wood, and the blocks were shaped so they would fit in the press. Emily and I hand-colored the illustrations, and each of the girls received her own personal copy. And again the Procession of the Candles was the memorable event of the day.

1532

February 23, 1532.   I have started to write down some of my special thoughts and beliefs concerning Jesus. Perhaps some day these can be incorporated into a book. The words flow effortlessly when I think of Jesus being with us in our everyday tasks.

March 28, 1532.   It has again been a long and bitter winter, and the cold cellar is nearly depleted. The smoked and salted meat from the butchering last fall is all but gone, but the chickens continue to produce fresh eggs. There is so very much to think of to provide for all the girls. But there has been so much activity in the instruction room this winter, no one else has had time to dwell on problems. With the printing press, library, weaving projects, art, song and prayer, our very large family is content.

April 8, 1532.   Just in time for Easter, Monsieur Estienne has sent up a new Bible, in French, translated from the Latin by Lefèvre d'Étaples at the University of Paris. This is wonderful, for it is the first time we can read the scriptures in French.

June 19, 1532.   Little Gregory, although no longer little for he is nine years of age, is already a great help to his father in the fields. But his real interest is in the press, and he would spend all day selecting type if we let him. Of course, now he is becoming a real charm to all of the girls.

June 22, 1532.   April made a large cake today in celebration of Sister Zoraida's birthday. We are all so thankful of how she has enriched our lives with her painting and weaving. The girls were all delighted with the surprise party.

October 17, 1532.   We have passed quietly through autumn, with the Orphanage running smoothly. We now have a full contingent of thirty-six girls. One additional sister has arrived from the Convent, and all is well.

December 25, 1532.   In addition to a new edition of special Christmas books for the girls, Emily and I have created a printed card for each of the people attending Mass. The card includes a printed excerpt from the Gospel by Luke on the Christmas Miracle, and an original greeting to all. The cards were treasured by all receiving them.

1533

January 17, 1533.   Michael and I discussed the state of France. He told me of the Peace of Chambray of several years ago, in which King Charles V and King Francis I had completed a treaty. "For the first time in many years, there is peace in the south of France and northern Italy," said Michael. "There are some very special places that I wish you could see. You are not cloistered, my dear sister. You provide service through an active life in the world. You need to see some of the wonders of our modern times."

"Are you proposing that I travel, Michael?"

"Yes, I am. Travel with me. In the name of the Orphanage and the Church, let us make a pilgrimage to Assisi."

Chapter 5
The Pilgrimage

February 8, 1533. Michael, Emily and I conferred with Bishop Briçonnet. Would he approve a pilgrimage to Assisi for Michael and me? We assured him the Orphanage would remain in good hands under Emily's direction. He knew of the good work Michael had done for King Francis, and agreed to speak to the King's Counsel on Michael's behalf. He seemed sure approval would be given.

February 17, 1533. Bishop Briçonnet has told us that he has sent word ahead to Father Gaetano de Thiene of our pilgrimage. Both he and Father Gaetano are members of the Oratory of Divine Love, he having come under its influence during his journey to Rome in 1522. The Oratory is a pious brotherhood dedicated to prayer, self-reform and service to the poor. We will meet Father Gaetano in either Assisi or Rome in June.

March 15, 1533. Plans are well underway for our journey. In recognition of Michael's faithful service in 1525 and 1526, and again in 1530, the King will

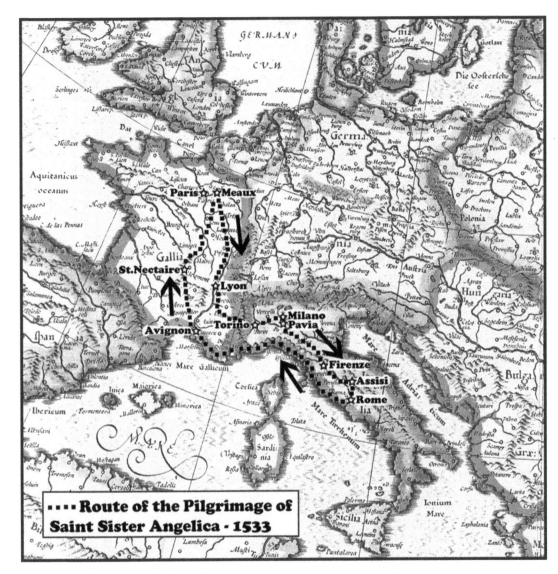

Route of the Pilgrimage, superimposed on a map by Mercator, circa 1590

sponsor the pilgrimage, and will send one of his aides to assist and be our protector and liaison. There are so many things that must be planned. Proper clothing to prepare, messages to send ahead, and most of all, horseback riding lessons for me. This is a vision, this is something I want to do. May God give me the courage to follow through.

April 5, 1533. Tomorrow we embark on our pilgrimage. We will be gone four months, or all of the summer. The girls are so sad to see me leave, but I promise them wonderful and sacred tales when I return. April is again with child, and the baby will probably be born before we return. But she said she will bear the chores cheerfully knowing we are at sacred shrines. Robert and Gregory have the garden and fields under full control.

April 6, 1533. Today we left at dawn. Father Leonard blessed us before we departed. There are new rose bushes next to the Church, and one early spring bloom sees us on our way. I wave to all the girls until they disappear from sight.

April 8 1533. This is all so new to me. We ride and ride and see more countryside than I ever imagined. There are people working the fields of their farms wherever we look. Tonight we are staying at the construction encampment at Chateau Fontainebleau. Hundreds of construction workers are enlarging this great Chateau for King Francis. Michael had visited this place several years ago, and can't believe his eyes at the new grandeur.

April 18 1533. It has taken us ten days to travel to Lyon. Today we visited the shop of several Italian potters, and how I wish I could take some of the intricate and colorful wares back to the Orphanage for careful examination. This could be another facet of study and instruction for the girls.

April 23, 1533. Several talented embroiderers were at the Convent of Lyon, but none nearly as good as at my Convent at L'Isle Adam (oh, it is so improper for me to think that, but it is true!). We have rested here for a week in a former military camp of King Francis. During the stay we toured the Roman ruins at Vienne, including a temple built in the reign of Emperor Claudius. I never thought I would see this monument as spoken about in one of the little books I read from the Estienne Publishing House.

May 3, 1533.   We have finally arrived in Torino. It was a very difficult ride over the Alps, but Michael kept promising me sunny skies and warmer days ahead. The Alps are a land where the snow never melts.

May 14, 1533.   We are now in Milano. Is this the beginning of the wonders of Italy that Michael has promised? Tomorrow we shall see.

May 15, 1533.   The visit to Tommaso Grassi's Free School for Poor Boys was enlightening. There are over three hundred boys in school here, receiving an education in reading, the arts, religion, and crafts. It is truly an inspiration for our Orphanage. There is also a hospital for the poor in Milano, where hundreds are fed and nursed every day. It is highly organized, with many of the trades represented right on the site. It is a second inspiration for our meager endeavors in Meaux. Never had I imagined the extending of such social benefits.

May 17, 1533.   Michael was playing a trick. He saved the best for our final days in Milano, for today we viewed the painting entitled Last Supper by Leonardo da Vinci at the Church of Santa Maria delle Grazie. Michael had seen this before, but I had forgotten his detailed description. Completed only thirty-three years ago, it is bright and fresh, vivid in style and color. The excited, agitated human gestures and questions directed to Jesus contrasts so with the repose seen in the divine face and figure of Jesus himself. How lofty the theme; what profound thoughts da Vinci must have carried with him for the years it took to complete the work. I felt all the time while viewing the work that I was being blessed, and that His presence was there in the room. If only this single spiritual moment comes from this pilgrimage, it has succeeded.

May 20, 1533. We had to leave Milano today, but I shall never forget the Last Supper. We are in Pavia, where Michael recalled the cold defeat of King Francis just eight years ago, and the ensuing detainment in Spain.

May 22, 1533. Oh, today we saw the wonderful Certosa! This old church has just been given a startling new façade of ornate marble. There are carvings of scrolls, shells, cherubs and cornucopias, and the towers at each end contain elaborate spirals and turrets. I made numerous sketches in my notebook, for I must remember this!

May 26, 1533. The city of Firenze was beautiful from the moment we arrived. There is marble and fountains and statues and stone architecture everywhere. Michael has learned that the great artist and sculptor Michel Angelo is presently working in this city, and Michael has requested an audience.

May 28, 1533. We met Michel Angelo today. He is a strong, robust man, fifty-eight years of age. He is working in the Medici Church of San Lorenzo, executing several giant marble statues for the tombs of the Medici family. His eyes were piercing, as those of a man who has seen great sights and visions. He inquired of the passing of his friend da Vinci fourteen years earlier in France. Other than these sculptures in progress, I have not yet seen any of his completed works.

May 30, 1533. Today we visited the Accademia, where we viewed the great sculpture called David. It is magnificent in height and color and shape. I must remind myself not to be offended by the nudity. The left arm is broken, but we were told it will be repaired yet this year.

Saint Francis as depicted in a stained glass window

June 4, 1533. I spent the entire day at the Biblioteca Laurenziana of San Lorenzo. The structure was designed by Michel Angelo, and it is sweeping and grand, although still not completed. The books in the temporary housing are marvelous, collected and published from all of the publishing houses. I viewed many hand-drawn manuscripts dating back a thousand years.

June 8, 1533. We are now on our way to Assisi, the objective of our pilgrimage. The days are tiring, but I am strengthened in our divine mission to capture the spirit of these holy places.

June 14, 1533. This has been our first day in Assisi. There are several groups of pilgrims here. We prayed at the little chapel of Saint Francis, the Portiuncula, and visited his tiny room on Mount Alvernus, where, after a vision, the marks of Jesus, the stigmata, appeared on his hands, feet and side.

June 16, 1533. All the while in Assisi both Michael and I sensed the supernatural presence of this holy place. We have asked for an audience with Brother Elias, General of the Order of Saint Francis.

June 17, 1533. Brother Elias is a very kind man, and he met with us and several other pilgrims this afternoon. Word of our coming had preceded us. He needed to know first hand of the account of the discovery of the relic of Saint Francis at the Orphanage chapel four years ago. He touched me gently as I told of the vision of light, and the finding. He said I was blessed, and asked me to join in the prayer of Saint Francis that completed his audience: "Let your behavior in the world be such that everyone who sees or hears you may praise the Heavenly Father. Preach peace to all; but have it in your hearts still more than on your lips. Give no occasion of anger or scandal to any, but by your gentleness lead all men to goodness, peace, and union."

June 20, 1533.   Today we had the privilege of meeting here in Assisi a very special person from Rome, Father Gaetano de Thiene du Caspar, member of the Oratory of Divine Love. We learned that the name Gaetano is Italian for the Latin name Cajetanus. Father Gaetano had been Superior of the Oratory until earlier this year. He also helped found the Order of Theatines, in which priests live under monastic rules of chastity, obedience and poverty. Father Gaetano is of noble lineage and once had great wealth, which has all been distributed to the poor. He says that his present mission is to root out the prevalent heretical teachings by the opponents of the Church. He said there is much work to do to cleanse the Church of improper conduct.

Father Gaetano and I talked privately for about an hour. I told him of my firm belief in Jesus and how I had been searching for Him in my prayers. Father Gaetano listened intently and suggested that I look to the beauty in all things and therein I may find answers to my questions. Father Gaetano will meet us again in Rome in a few days.

June 25, 1533.   Our pilgrimage is nearing its completion, for we are now in Rome. We still see scars of the destruction done by the army of King Charles V just five years ago. Rome is a quaint mixture of ruins—ruins of ancient Roman arches and fortifications, ruins of recent wars, and ruins of old structures being demolished and rebuilt, such as St. Peter's Basilica, where four great pillars of the new church are already standing.

June 27, 1533.   Michel Angelo said that we would like it, and we did. Today we visited the Sistine Chapel, and studied the great ceiling that took the artist four years to complete. The fresco tells the story of Genesis even more vividly than the scripture. There are five great Creation panels, all looming down from a pure blue sky. The most inspiring scene depicts God stretching out a divine finger, touching the timid fingertip of the creature, Adam, whom he has just created. Oh, so much beauty is here. Such an inspired person Michel Angelo is. I would hope that some day all the girls of the Orphanage could meet him and see his great works.

June 29, 1533.   We have again met Father Gaetano and he led us on a tour of Rome. I was most overwhelmed by the Pietá, a sensitive sculpture by Michel Angelo, depicting Jesus in His mother's arms. It is exquisite, precious, and beautiful. Presently it is in the private courtyard of Pope Clement VII (Giulio de Medici), awaiting the completion of the new Saint Peter's Basilica. Father Gaetano has worked closely with Pope Clement outlining the need and methods of reform in the Church, and has proposed a Council of Bishops to define carefully Church dogma.

July 1, 1533.   After a day of rest, today we performed the pilgrimage around Rome with Father Gaetano. As was customary, we visited the seven major churches in the city in one day. I was exhausted, for, in addition, we fasted so that we might receive Communion at the end of the circuit. It was a wonderful and holy day.

July 9, 1533.   We have completed our visit to Rome, and bade a fond farewell to Father Gaetano. He told us to visit again the Church of Santa Maria in Milano, where we might participate in a new ceremony called the Forty Hours' Devotion. The Devotion had just been approved by Pope Clement. He wished us well in our journey north, and hopes that we can meet again, if not in this world, certainly in the next.

July 20, 1533.   We are again in Milano. While retracing our steps to view one more time the Last Supper, we were invited by the Deacon to participate in the new Forty Hours' Devotion. We were astonished at its simplicity, and inspired by its intent. For forty consecutive hours prayers are said before the Blessed Sacrament, in memory of the forty hours during which the Sacred Body of Jesus was in the

Saint-Nectaire Church, Saint-Nectaire-le Haut, France

sepulcher. The Blessed Sacrament is exposed in the form of a consecrated host in an elaborate Monstrance. It is surrounded by hundreds of candles which create an air of sanctity and beauty.

I spent several hours in the Devotion, praying and meditating. All the time I felt the presence of Jesus, for He was there in the presence of the Eucharist. "This wonderful Devotion we must bring back to the Orphanage, and the Church of Saint Francis of Assisi," I thought. Later I spoke to the Deacon to get all the particulars of the ritual, as authorized by Pope Clement.

July 30, 1533. We have taken a more southerly route home, traveling through Provence. Here in Avignon we have toured the Cathedral and Palace of the Popes, official seat of the Church in the mid 1300s. The lower Rhone River Valley is the most beautiful I can imagine—a visual paradise—now in its full summer glory.

August 5–7, 1533. We are resting for several days at the priory next to the Saint-Nectaire church. This impressive stone church was built about 300 years ago on a hilltop near the small town founded by the Romans. It contains a treasury of art and was named for the missionary Saint Nectaire. Here I prayed for our safe return to the orphanage.

August 16, 1533. Home. The Orphanage. How beautiful it all looked as we rounded the bend in the road and saw the Church for the first time in over four months. I am exhausted beyond measure, and must rest to regain my strength. The girls were all so excited to see our return. Our family has grown by one, little John, born a month ago to April and Robert. There are so many stories to tell, so many wonders to explain. And so many prayers to be said for fulfillment of the visions of the pilgrimage. Oh, Michael, my wonderful brother Michael, how can I thank you for your persistence in convincing me this pilgrimage would be worthwhile, and your patience during these more than four months?

Chapter 6
Forty Hours' Devotion

August 30, 1533. I have met with Bishop Briçonnet and delivered the greeting sent by Father Gaetano. The Bishop was particularly thrilled to hear of the Forty Hours' Devotion. "It would be most appropriate for us to conduct this Devotion here in this Diocese at the Church of Saint Francis of Assisi," he said. "You select the day, and I will be present to initiate it."

September 17, 1533. This is the Feast of the Stigmata of Saint Francis, and the first day of the first Forty Hours' Devotion in all of France. The Church was beautifully decorated, and the area of the altar was draped in white to bring full attention to the Eucharist. Emily had printed a brochure explaining the meaning of the Devotion, and included a number of prayers and psalms for those attending the opening or any time during the service. It is required that at least two people be present in the Church at all times that the Sacred Body is exposed. The girls were more than anxious at taking their turn at "watching over Jesus" as they called it. The Bishop inspired all of us with his opening words concerning the presence of Jesus.

September 19, 1533. The Devotion is complete, and all received much inspiration during their hours of visitation. We have decided that the Devotion should be conducted every six months, or whenever special prayers are needed.

December 25, 1533. It was so beautiful to view the Procession of the Candles again, and see our large family together. Sister Johnetta surprised us this year with a special Christmas chorus, with songs sung from books sent up by Monsieur Estienne. Near the end of the service sunlight flickered through the round window above the altar, sending colored rays down on the congregation. And once again the cards were taken home as treasures by all attending.

December 31, 1533. This is the close of a wonderful year, a year of great growth for me. I hope I can fulfill all the plans that the pilgrimage inspired.

1534

January 24, 1534. This is a very sad moment. Word has been received that Bishop Briçonnet suddenly took ill several days ago, and today he passed away. He was such a strong man, wishing for reform in the Church and allowing free thinking to take place without damaging the Church. We do not know what will become of the Orphanage. We will need a new sponsor, for we are not self-sufficient. The Orphanage has many, many friends, but none who have expressed interest in sponsorship. The word will soon get out of our plight, and we shall see what God has in mind for us.

January 27, 1534. There was a great Requiem Mass for Bishop Briçonnet at the Meaux Cathedral. Many clergy from Paris attended, and the choir sang as if from heaven.

February 18, 1534.   Through the generosity of the neighbors and patrons from Meaux, we are able to sustain ourselves through spring, but after that we are unsure. We must trust in God that we will be able to continue our mission.

March 21, 1534.   The second Forty Hours' Devotion has been held. Father Leonard began the service two days ago, in honor or Bishop Briçonnet. To my surprise, an elaborate gold Monstrance was delivered before the start of the Devotion. The Monstrance was commissioned by Bishop Briçonnet before his death, and delivered by one of his former aides. Special hymns, which filled our hearts with love, were sung at the closing. The hymns were arranged by Sister Johnetta.

May 18, 1534.   The spring planting is completed, and tending the garden has begun. We continue to have hope for our future.

July 5, 1534.   Donations continue to arrive from unknown sources. The fame of the Orphanage has spread throughout Paris, and many people have inquired as to how they can assist us.

September 17, 1534.   The Forty Hours' Devotion is now eagerly anticipated by everyone. The opening remarks this time were delivered by a visiting scholar from Paris, Ignatius Loyola, who has just completed his studies in philosophy and divinity at the University of Paris. He spoke of his own experiences and trials—that of a wounded soldier, his intense reading of the Life of the Lord and the Lives of the Saints, and his vision of Our Lady. He spoke of how peace comes to his mind and body through holy thoughts; but unrest and discontent come with worldly thoughts. He concluded with: "Receive, O Lord, all my liberty, my memory, my understanding and my will. You have given me all that I possess, and I surrender all to Your Divine Will. Give me only Your love and Your grace. With this I am rich enough." Everyone was moved to tears with the strength of his words.

A monstrance as used in the Forty Hours' Devotion to display the Eucharist

December 25, 1534.   Again we celebrated the Birth of Jesus, contemplating true faith and devotion. The vision created by the Procession of the Candles once again confirmed that the Orphanage has succeeded only through His Will.

1535

January 24, 1535.   This winter, I am writing in earnest my thoughts concerning Jesus. I think it is necessary to put my innermost feelings on paper.

March 19, 1535.   For the spring Forty Hours' Devotion we invited another guest to open the ceremony, at the recommendation of Ignatius Loyola. Francis Xavier studied with Ignatius Loyola, and together they have founded a community called the Society of Jesus, which is dedicated to reform of the Church through education, frequent taking of the sacraments, and zealous missionary work. "It is Jesus living in you that makes all things possible. It is this intimacy with our Lord here on earth, in the midst of all suffering, that gives us strength," were his concluding remarks. Once again we were in tears.

May 19, 1535.   A familiar visitor has arrived, Monsieur Henri Estienne. He was so excited to see the work we have done with the old printing press. He was especially charmed by the cards of greeting we deliver at Christmas. "Sister Angelica," he started, "could you, Emily and Sister Zoraida develop a set of these for me? Could you write the messages and design the images? I could take them to my publishing house and perhaps they could become popular throughout Paris during the Christmas season. I know the Orphanage is in search of a patron, and I would promise you continued support for this one favor."

"Oh, of course we can do it," I replied. "The girls are always so full of ideas, we can hardly record them all. And Gregory is so much help with the designs created by Sister Zoraida and crafted by Eulogio. It will be a fine project for the Orphanage."

We continued to discuss the proposal through the evening, and Monsieur enjoyed the night as guest of the Orphanage.

May 20, 1535.   "There are several other dreams I have," I continued the next morning. "The pilgrimage of two years ago showed me so much."

"What did you see that inspired you, Sister Angelica?" he asked.

"In Milano there is a school and orphanage for several hundred children," I replied. "Our operation here is tiny by comparison, and there is such a great need to tend to the children. That is one of my great wishes, to expand the Orphanage."

"And another wish, Sister?"

"A bell tower. A tower soaring into the sky, with many bells that would chime out on the hour and before Mass and whenever there is need for prayer. I saw first hand the Certosa in Pavia. I have some sketches." I ran to the study to retrieve my notebook. "Look at these details. Aren't they magnificent?" I stumbled all over myself with excitement. "We could design the bell tower with all these scrolls and carvings. It would be the focal point of the Orphanage."

"And still another wish, Sister?"

"Yes, one more. Time to write and print my thoughts. And find other sisters to whom I could express my feelings and who might want to follow some of my thinking. My head just bursts with ideas sometimes."

"This is a lot to ask in exchange for just a few verses and designs for cards of greeting," he replied, quite sternly. But he did have a twinkle in his eye, and I knew we had a new beginning. "But just one wish at a time," he cautioned.

Chapter 7
A New Beginning

June 20, 1535.   An architect has arrived from Paris, sent up by Monsieur Estienne, and designs are beginning for tripling the size of the dormitory and instruction room. Emily, Robert, and April, and everyone else in the family, are so excited. We all conferred around large sheets of paper, and we each scribbled down our ideas. The architect was amazed at our enthusiasm, and was quickly swept up by our sincerity.

September 3, 1535.   The plans are complete, and Monsieur Estienne himself arrived for the ground breaking. Father Leonard came in from Meaux on this special day, and after special meditation in the Church, we assembled at the far corner of the area where the new dormitory was to be built. Oh, how useful it will be.

September 17, 1535.   The autumn Forty Hours' Devotion was opened by Father Peter Favre, an associate of both Ignatius Loyola and Francis Xavier, and a member of the Society of Jesus. He was ordained a priest last year, and spoke of the blessings that are all around us, if only we take a moment to see them in our daily lives.

September 21, 1535.   Word has arrived that the Town Land Steward has donated additional land to the Orphanage. This will mean more land for orchards, gardens, grain and stables.

September 30, 1535.   All this month it was necessary to think of Christmas, since Monsieur Estienne needed the verses and designs by today so that they could be ready by early December. We all assisted in selecting the ones we wished to send, and we will hold the other ideas over for next year.

December 25, 1535.   The Procession of the Candles was especially beautiful this year, for we prayed in thanks for the ongoing construction of the significant enlargement of all our facilities, and the knowledge that soon there would be many more children to benefit from our work.

1536

February 17, 1536.   The new dormitory has risen steadily all this winter, for it has been mild without much snow. The laborers stay at the site during the week, but return to their homes on Saturday so they can attend Mass with their families on Sunday. There are many more mouths to feed, but April has energies far beyond our expectation. Perhaps she gets her energy from her little son John who is always tumbling about her feet.

March 21, 1536.   Once more the Forty Hours' Devotion was a great success. The visitors saw the new enthusiasm in all of us as the new dormitory takes shape. Our guest was again Ignatius Loyola, who inspired us with his wisdom. He will depart from Paris next week on a mission to Spain.

September 25, 1536. The new dormitory is complete, and our Forty Hours' Devotion was held in thanks for this small miracle. I expect that Sister Agatha will soon be sending several more girls to share in our wealth of family. Our guest speaker to open the Devotion was our special friend, Monsieur Henri Estienne. In keeping with the religious theme, he spoke of the dedicated theologians at the Sorbonne with whom he has worked while preparing their manuscripts for publishing. It opened the eyes of all of us as to the intense study that is now going on in an effort to protect the teachings and mission of the Church.

October 19, 1536. I was correct, and three more girls arrived today. Word is spreading throughout Paris of our great accomplishments.

December 25, 1536. We have all worked tirelessly this year, and once more we enjoy the spiritual fulfillment we all find on Christmas Day in the Church.

1537

February 19, 1537. The architect is here again! He himself had toured northern Italy only last year, and saw the Certosa. He brought drawings that showed what he had in mind for the bell tower, but our design group added many more flourishes and mini-spires. "Monsieur Estienne has employed a bell maker from Rennes, and the sounds will bring glory to all living in this region," he said. And then he continued with the fantastic news. "Through his friendship with King Francis, two stone carvers relocated from the Chateau Fontainebleau will be assigned to supervise the carving of the façade itself. It will be everything you had imagined, and more."

"The orientation," I said, "is something we must discuss. In my sleep I saw a tower at a special angle to the Church. Not centered, not square, but at an offset angle.

Let me show you where it must be." We stepped outside in the light snow. Upon approaching the Church, we all stopped in amazement.

"Who put these marks in the snow?" Michael asked.

"This is new snow, and I haven't been here," I replied. But the snow marks coincided exactly with the location of the tower as seen in my dream.

"Yes, we have had occurrences here before," Michael said, and then with set determination exclaimed, "and this is the location of the tower."

March 21, 1537. We are awaiting the final drawings, delivery of materials, and arrival of the stone carvers for the bell tower. To this we have dedicated our spring Forty Hours' Devotion.

July 19, 1537. The bell tower is well underway. The foundation is in place, and the stone carvers have recruited a number of local workmen to be trained to assist in the carving. Already there is a small field of carved panels, just waiting for installation.

September 19, 1537. The Forty Hours' Devotion coincided with the delivery of the bells, even though it will be months before there will be a place to install them. The opening remarks of the Devotion were made by Carolyn, one of the older girls who has been here the longest. She spoke clearly and assuredly of her ten years at the Orphanage, her sense of security, and the knowledge she has attained, all through the grace of God. We were all so very proud of her.

September 30, 1537. Our month again has been busy thinking of Christmas designs and messages. It is like having the spirit of Christmas with us for several months of the year, and we all enjoy the challenge of capturing the correct divine message.

December 25, 1537.   The entire congregation sang lovely songs from printed sheets created by Sister Johnetta. This is the first time we reproduced printed music, copied from a new songbook supplied by Monsieur Estienne.

December 28, 1537.   Today we had a surprise party for Eulogio. It is his birthday, and all the girls wanted to show him special thanks for the furniture he has made and the carvings he has created. To help celebrate the occasion, Robert brought in some rich red wine that he has produced from the grapes in the vineyard.

1538

March 18, 1538.   The bell tower is complete, and the bells will ring out for the first time at the opening of the Devotion. Monsieur Estienne is here for the dedication, and the sight of the bell tower brought tears to his eyes. It is so beautiful. The stone carvings are a series of scrolls up all four sides, interlaced with small crosses, and four archways outlining niches in which are placed four statues of early saints.

March 19, 1538.   The bells have tolled for the first time, and what a magnificent sound they make. They are firm yet sweet as honey. They are a joy to hear, and they sing out in mellow tones across the landscape, like voices. The unique orientation causes the notes to reflect from the walls of the Church. What a wonderful gift to the Orphanage. All of Paris will want to come to see the bell tower and have the bells sound in their ears. Gregory had a wonderful time assisting in pulling the ropes, and I think he will soon become our official bell master.

March 21, 1538.   This was a special Devotion, for we incorporated the tolling of the bells into the service every two hours. The entire region herewith knew of the exhibition of the Blessed Sacrament and the Holy Presence that was within the walls of the Church.

May 30, 1538.　Fifty-three girls are now at the Orphanage, and at times our resources are strained. We need more instructors, and I have sent Mother Superior a plea for more assistance.

June 19, 1538.　It has been five years since I've been away from the Orphanage and Meaux, and Michael, Emily and I have decided to travel to Paris for several days. We will be the guests of Monsieur Estienne.

June 25, 1538.　As in the old days, we floated down the Marne River into the heart of Paris. What memories flooded through our minds, thinking of Mama and Papa twenty years ago when we floated back from our grand summer holiday with Grandmama and Grandpapa.

June 26, 1538.　So much has changed. Things seem smaller, yet larger at the same time. We learned that our dear friend Sister Agatha had suddenly passed away. There is so much disease in the city. Our rooms of the past are all gone. The only familiar landmark is the Cathedral of Notre Dame. It is so much larger than I remember. Perhaps that is because of my constant exposure to our own Church of Saint Francis of Assisi, which is very small in comparison.

June 27, 1538.　Monsieur Estienne gave us a complete tour of the Publishing House. It is now four times as large as it was when I first experienced the scent of newly printed books, all neatly arranged on the shelves. He made gifts to all of us of several new publications.

June 29, 1538.　We traveled to the Convent to renew old acquaintances. It has been twelve years since I left, yet it seems like yesterday. Everything is the same—the rooms, the chapel, and even the library. Hardly anything new has been added. Certainly someone could have thought of continued revitalization, but apparently no one has. "Why weren't there other sisters who sought the gift of knowledge?"

Mother Superior could not answer this question. "You were always special, Sister Angelica," she said, "and brought out ourselves in us. No one like you has been here since."

Mother Superior and I had a long, private conversation concerning the things to come that I had in my mind. It was a wonderful day—a day where an additional purpose in my life was set.

July 2, 1538. Once again we are back at the Orphanage. Monsieur Estienne was a perfect host while we were in Paris. We have so much for which to extend gratitude to him. I have returned to the Orphanage with renewed vigor to set out on an expanded course.

Chapter 8
Confraternity of the Divine Presence

July 8, 1538.   The summer is wonderful. The fields are green, the flowers are blooming, and the birds are singing. I have made myself a special outside work area so I can be close to the things that I love, and see all of our accomplishments. I have taken to studying my diary and private writings that started so many years ago, concerning my beliefs in Jesus.

July 15, 1538.   Today was a blessed day, for I was asked a very simple question by René, our new nine-year-old girl. She walked up to me in my outside study and sat down, wondering what I was doing. I said I was reviewing my thoughts of Jesus that I had written in my notebooks. René asked, "Where do I find Jesus?"

My words just flowed out, for the first time. "You find Jesus all around you. Jesus is here in the bright green trees, in the blue sky, in the birds and butterflies, in the puppies and kittens, in the grain in the fields and the cows in the stable, and He is here too," I said, poking her gently in her ribs. She squealed with delight.

"But Sister Johnette has read us the Christmas story many times," she replied, "and I have read it myself. Saint Luke described the birth of Jesus as it happened over fifteen hundred years ago. How could Jesus still be here today? He'd be so old!"

"Oh, but He is here, René. Jesus, and the spirit of Jesus, is more than a thirty-three year span of time oh so many years ago. He continues to live with us every day. Just look at that beautiful spider web all filled with dew. Just look at the clouds reflected in the bird bath. Just look at that clump of white daisies. Just look at the kind thoughts in your heart. His presence is all around. You do not have to look high and low to search Him out, for He is right here."

July 16, 1538.   News travels quickly around the Orphanage. Two other girls approached me today to hear my story of the Presence of Jesus all around us. I told them to gather all the girls into the Church that evening after supper, for I had even more thoughts to relate, as connecting thoughts occurred to me from the Holy Bible.

I started the evening story by repeating what I had told René the day before. "But there is more," I continued. "Look at what it says here in the Bible, written by Saint Luke, in 17:24: 'For behold, the Kingdom of God is within you.' Saint Matthew also recalled Jesus as saying, 'Behold, I am with you all days.' Jesus also said, "Where two or three are gathered in my name, there am I in the midst of them.' So you see, my dear children, Jesus does live with us at all times." There were many questions, and I tried to answer them the best I could. When a child speaks, she speaks from the heart. We closed the evening with the poem I composed many years ago which we all had memorized:

Thank You Lord:
For each new day you give to me,
For earth and sky and sand and sea;
For rainbows after springtime showers,
Autumn leaves and summer flowers;
For winter snowscapes so serene,
Harvest fields of gold and green;
For beauty shining all around;
Lilac scent and robin sound;
For stars that twinkle high above,
And all the people that I love.
Amen.

July 30, 1538.   I have been struggling all week with a letter to Mother Superior concerning my wishes to come to the Convent to express my new heartfelt beliefs. Although we had spoken of these thoughts in general a month ago, I felt it was now time I must act. At last my message to her is off.

August 5, 1538.   Mother Superior has invited me to return to the Convent to speak to the sisters of my beliefs and plans. I will leave as quickly as possible.

August 20, 1538.   I have arrived at the Convent, full of hope in my mission.

August 22, 1538.   After a day of prayer, I was ready. "I have a special prayer and plea to all of you," I began, after assembling many of the sisters, old and young, in the chapel. "Let us read Psalm 103 together."

And so we read: "Bless the Lord, O my soul! ... You make the clouds your chariot; you travel on the wings of the wind ... You send forth springs into the watercourses that wind among the mountains ...beside them the birds of heaven dwell; from among the branches they send forth their song ... You made the moon to mark the seasons; the sun knows the hour of its setting ... how manifold are Your works, O

Lord! ... may the glory of the Lord endure forever ... I will sing praise to my God while I live, pleasing to Him be my theme; I will be glad in the Lord ... Bless the Lord, O my soul! Alleluia."

I continued with the stories of the Presence of Jesus that I had told to the girls in the Church. "I believe so deep in my heart that Jesus the Lord is with us always, and He is manifest in all living things. He gives us life every day. He lets us sing His praises."

"I would like to found a Confraternity to foster this belief in all who would listen. We shall call it the Confraternity of the Divine Presence. Who of you will join me?"

There was a wonderful glow in the eyes of a number of the sisters. "We will follow your thoughts and examples, Sister Angelica," they announced together. "There is good work being done by many today who are away as missionaries," continued Sister Rebecca. "We could continue similar work in and around Paris."

"And perhaps even farther," added Sister Ruth Anne.

"I will set up a meeting with the Bishop of Saint Denis to discuss our plans," said Mother Superior. "I know he will be pleased, for he has spoken often of additional good work we could do in the name of Jesus. We just didn't know where to start. Thank you, Sister Angelica!"

August 31, 1538. The Bishop was indeed pleased. "We need to write down all the thoughts, and develop a plan for us to jointly follow," he said to Mother Superior and me. "Please stay with us here at the Convent as long as you can—you have my full support."

September 16, 1538. Today at last I returned to the Orphanage. The Bishop traveled with me to open this Forty Hours' Devotion. He spoke of my plans to found the Confraternity of the Divine Presence, and we dedicated the entire Devotion to its success. All of the older girls are thrilled to be so close to this grand plan, and even the little girls, too young to understand, shared in the excitement. And my extended family—Emily and Michael, April and Robert, Gregory and John, Sister Johnetta, Sister Zoraida, and Eulogio—could see in my new spirited ways that something special had come over me.

November 25, 1538.   I have spent nearly half the time during the past two months at the Convent conferring with Mother Superior, and with her assistance we have outlined an entire course of study and devotion which will become the framework of the Confraternity. All my writings of the past have been very useful. In our more excited moments we would speculate as to how the word would be spread—how we would go out into the parishes and streets to work with the mothers and fathers and children—to spread the word of the Divine Presence. At times during these weeks we became like children ourselves. But after this intense period I needed to return to the Orphanage to gain strength that I find in the family, the girls, and our own Church of Saint Francis of Assisi.

December 16, 1538.   Six of the sisters from the Convent, all who show a very devout interest in becoming the first members of the Confraternity, have arrived here at the Orphanage to spend the Christmas Season with us. They were thrilled to meet all the girls, and pray in the Church. Oh, our Procession of the Candles will be very special this year.

December 25, 1538.   The songs filled our hearts. The message of Jesus became even more clear to us as we contemplated the strength of our own faith. I joined hand in hand with our six visiting sisters and we each felt a presence of faith, love and hope from within. Our special purpose will be successful.

1539

January 9, 1539. Tomorrow I must leave again for the Convent, with the six sisters, so we can begin our dedicated period of instruction in the Confraternity. The plan set out by Mother Superior and me calls for a study time of three months. After supper tonight we joined together in the Church for contemplation and prayer. From Psalm 104 we read: "Give thanks to the Lord, invoke His name; make known among the nations His deeds. Sing to Him, sing His praise, proclaim all His wondrous deeds. Look to the Lord in His strength; seek to serve Him constantly. ... And He led forth His people with joy; with shouts of joy. Alleluia."

March 19, 1539. It is the Feast of Saint Joseph, and our small group, those fervently dedicated to the founding of the Confraternity, began at sunset our own Forty Hours' Devotion in the Convent chapel.

March 21, 1539. By the completion of the Devotion, all of the Convent sisters had joined in the celebration of the Presence of Jesus. It was my first Devotion away from the Orphanage since first we started it six years ago. But, oh, what rewards are coming through the flowing of grace of the Lord during this special time.

April 20, 1539. How appropriate that our three months of study should be completed during Holy Week. We are especially thankful for the understanding we have reached within ourselves, the principles of our new beliefs, and our intent to share the principles of the Confraternity with all who will listen. The Bishop of Saint Denis conferred a special prayer and blessing over all of us today, to sanctify our Confraternity.

May 1, 1539. Once again I have returned to the Orphanage. How happy I was to see all my special friends again, and to meditate quietly within the grounds of my true home.

May 15, 1539.   There is much organizational work that must be done, and I shall travel again to Paris so our work can begin.

June 7, 1539.   With the aid of the sisters at the Cathedral of Notre Dame, and in the memory of Sister Agatha, we have begun to work with members of several local parishes. Already several of the sisters here wish to become members of the Confraternity, but they must wait until after the next instruction period next spring. I do not know how to show my grateful appreciation for their assistance; they are remembered sincerely in my prayers.

July 9, 1539.   The illness in this city of Paris is very sad. So many children are left without parents, and parents without their children. It is so difficult to preach the Presence of Jesus in the midst of such human turmoil. When I am with such a group we try to find solace together in the Psalms. From Psalm 12: "How long, O Lord, will you utterly forget me? How long will you hide your face from me? How long shall I harbor sorrow in my soul, grief in my heart day after day … Give light to my eyes that I may not sleep in death … Let my heart rejoice in your salvation; let me sing of the Lord, 'He has been good to me.'"

September 17, 1539.   A small group of us, along with a number of special friends in Jesus that have been listening to our message, have agreed to conduct a Forty Hours' Devotion in the far chapel of the Cathedral. It was wonderful to see the fulfillment in their eyes as the Devotion progressed.

September 29, 1539.   We have been working day and night in the streets of Paris, and are beginning to see understanding in the eyes of the people we have met and to whom we have preached and shared our word. But how I long for the Orphanage! I must return there soon to regain my strength of mind and purpose.

October 30, 1539.   At last I am again at the Orphanage, and refreshment swept over me the moment I spied the bell tower. The two treasures of the Orphanage are now Gregory, who is a young man of sixteen, and John, who is already six. Although Gregory quite dutifully assists his father in the fields, he also has all but taken over the press, and knows every quirk of its machinery. Little John, in the meantime, is forever chasing the geese and the chickens, but does assist with the chores in the dairy. April and Robert know he will grow out of his mischief making.

December 25, 1539. The Church was filled with visitors from Meaux to witness the Procession of the Candles, and to hear all the girls participate in songs conducted by Sister Johnetta. The Church rang with their sweet voices, and the great Angel in Blue looked down with pleasure. The light from the hundreds of flickering candles mixed with the beam of golden light from the circular window to create a special glow in my heart.

December 29, 1539. Michael has arrived with incredibly exciting news. King Charles of Spain, Emperor of the Holy Roman Empire, has become very cordial with King Francis. King Charles is to visit Paris for a short time in January, and King Francis proposed that King Charles visit Meaux and the Orphanage to see the great humanitarian work that is being done here. As soon as the rest heard this news, the entire Orphanage became a buzz of preparation.

1540

January 2, 1540. I have notified Mother Superior that the beginning of the instruction in the Confraternity must be delayed until early February because of the royal visit. Everyone here is beyond themselves in anticipation.

January 7, 1540. Three people from the advance party of King Charles have arrived to assist in preparation. They conferred with everyone who in the remotest way was participating in the preparation.

January 12, 1540. The tour of the Orphanage by King Charles was grand and magnificent. The bells in the tower tolled out his arrival loud and majestically. He showed immense interest in the large dormitory and instruction room for the girls, and Gregory proudly displayed the printing press and many of the books, cards and song sheets that the press had printed. He especially admired the carved illustration blocks for the press created by Sister Zoraida and Eulogio. He was overwhelmed by the simplicity, and yet great beauty, of the Church, with its stained glass and carved decorations. He stared for quite some time at the Angel in Blue. He was treated to a simple but satisfying feast prepared and overseen by April, and even asked for a second helping of April's famous flatcakes. He was charmed by all the girls, and delighted in their self-confidence, knowledge and grace.

After the feast, gifts were exchanged. As soon as we heard of the impending visit by King Charles, all the sisters and the older girls took turns working day and night on a small embroidered tapestry designed by Sister Zoraida depicting a panorama of the grounds of the Orphanage. Several girls were shown playing in the foreground, and King Charles was most delighted with the personal gift. In turn he presented the Orphanage with a satchel of hard yellow grain seed. He said rare kernels of this type were first brought back by Cristoforo Colombo in 1493 from the voyage to the west, where the natives called it mahiz. It has been grown successfully in the fields of Spain, yielding a four-foot plant with long cones totally surrounded in rows by these yellow kernels, which in turn would each grow new plants, or could be ground into a meal for cooking. Robert was truly delighted with this gift to try in the fields, and April was anxious to try the ground meal in her kitchen.

King Charles expressed a great deal of thanks for the hospitality he was shown before he departed for the evening to Meaux and the Bishop's residence. As the tower bells proclaimed his departure, we all sensed a great deal of emptiness, for he was very gracious and warm.

February 15, 1540.   A large group of new sisters has assembled at the Convent to begin instruction into the Confraternity. I will participate during the entire time, to assure conformance with the principles as set down.

March 21, 1540.   We broke the instruction again this year with the Forty Hours' Devotion, in which everyone participated. Our work in the name of the Lord is finding great rewards.

June 3, 1540.   The completion of the instruction is behind us, and groups of sisters have gone to both Paris and farther south to Orléans. Michael has arrived here at the Convent to accompany me back to Meaux.

June 17, 1540.   It has been a wonderful two weeks of meditation and being with my family. But once again I yearn for the association with the other sisters of the Confraternity, and the faces of the people who hear the word we are preaching. So I must be off once again to Paris.

July 9, 1540.   The situation here is so sad, and there is so much to do. We work tirelessly in the name of Jesus. All of the sisters of the Confraternity show a great deal of energy in their pursuits. A letter has arrived from Orléans detailing the success of spreading the message in that city.

September 8, 1540.   In the company of Michael, I have arrived in Orléans to assist the sisters of the Confraternity here. We all met with the Bishop, and he consented to support our cause. He is so surprised that a group of sisters could have such spiritual zeal. Several of the local sisters here have shown interest in becoming members of the Confraternity.

September 19, 1540.   Together we have conducted our Forty Hours' Devotion in a chapel adjacent to the Cathedral. A number of local people joined us and once again experienced an elation at the end of the Devotion brought on by the continued Presence of Jesus.

November 3, 1540.   My time in Orléans has come to a close and I will leave for Paris tomorrow. Much great work has been done here.

December 25, 1540.   The girls are so wonderful in their song and devotion on this memorable day. I am so thankful to Emily, April and Robert for continuing to foster and expand the great work here at the Orphanage. But I am taken by strange melancholic thoughts that fill my mind, and the Spirit of the Season is not with me this year.

December 27, 1540.   I met privately with Gregory, such a fine young man. He put his arm around my shoulder as I told him of my sadness which seems to have no cause. We sat together in silence, and then, as if guided by some external force, he said, "Sister Angelica, your writings need to reach a wider audience. Let us work together to set down your thinking onto the printed page. It would please me very much to work these cold winter days in the light of your wisdom and the service of your mission."

I hugged him. "Oh yes, Gregory. What a wonderful idea. Let us begin very quickly. I have copies of all my notes right here."

1541

January 8, 1541.   Gregory and I have been working for nearly two weeks without stopping, arranging my writings into essays. Gregory is a very intelligent man, and quickly grasps the meaning of my words and rearranges my random writing into an organized flow of thoughts and prayers. We work perfectly together, and I forever shall cherish this union.

January 10, 1541. Tomorrow I must leave for the Convent, and the beginning of the new instruction period. The entire Confraternity will assemble for the first three days to renew our mission and principles. Gregory has promised to work on the printing project during my absence.

March 21, 1541. The Forty Hours' Devotion renews all of us in our quest to seek the Presence of Jesus in all things.

April 9, 1541. A courier arrived quite unannounced this morning from the Estienne Publishing House. He brought a large package, and said it must be delivered to me personally. Mother Superior was there when I tore it open. Inside the package were twenty copies of a small volume, bound in dark blue leather, embossed in gold with the title:

The Blessed Thoughts
of
Sister Angelica
Founder of the
Confraternity of the Divine Presence

Accompanying the volumes was a short note from Monsieur Estienne:

"April 7, 1541

"Dear Sister Angelica,

"Several weeks ago I received twenty sets of printed sheets from Gregory from the Orphanage. He requested that I assemble these sheets into bound volumes, which I have just completed today with much pleasure. You have put so many beautiful thoughts into words, and I thank you for the honor of being able to play a small role in their publishing."

If Mother Superior hadn't been there to catch me, I would have fainted.

April 10, 1541.   It took me a full day to regain my composure. Finally today I was able to write a note of thanks and appreciation to both Gregory and Monsieur Henri Estienne.

April 20, 1541.   The instruction period was completed today, and all of the members of the Confraternity, now numbering nineteen, renewed our Vows and were blessed by the Bishop of Saint Denis. I presented each one of them with a copy of "Blessed Thoughts".

April 23, 1541.   A most unusual letter arrived today at the Convent. It reads:

"April 7, 1541

"My dear Sister Angelica,

"Today I found on the desk in my study here in Naples a copy of your 'Blessed Thoughts.' It is a most wonderful publication, and poignantly reflects the thoughts you expressed when we met in the spring of 1533 in both Assisi and Rome. How delighted I was to read your words, and feel the inner personal commitment you have to the Presence of Jesus.

"I have been negligent in not writing you earlier, for I heard some months ago of your fine work and the founding of the Confraternity of the Divine Presence via a message from the Bishop of Saint Denis. This is a brave and honorable endeavor, and I am confident the grace of the Lord is with you.

"I wish we could speak together in person regarding the great need for work of the type you are doing, in these trying times for the Church. It is a time of necessary reforms, and you are courageous to carry the banner. Your letter rings hope into my soul, and joy in the present and trust in the future. May you feel renewed once again that He who did not fail you in the past will not fail you in the future. Know that He will not try you beyond your strength.

"I know not how I received your volume, for no courier brought it, nor was there a message attached. But I thank the Lord for such a blessing on this day.

> "Yours in devotion to Jesus,
> "Father Gaetano de Thiene du Caspar
> "Naples."

As soon as I realized that Father Gaetano's letter carried the same date as Monsieur Estienne's note, I ran to chapel to be with the Lord.

May 3, 1541.   I have stayed on until now at the Convent, for I continue to sense a strange mystery around me. I care not to speak of visions, but there is a sense of wonder in my heart. Mother Superior has listened, but even she cannot comprehend what I feel.

May 8, 1541.   Michael has arrived to accompany me to the Orphanage. When we first caught sight of the bell tower, we both noticed an unusual quietness about the grounds. In fact, no one was to be seen outside, and such a sunny spring day it was. We approached the instruction room, and as we opened the door the room burst into greetings of "Happy Birthday" by everyone from my family and all of the girls. Oh, how surprised I was! What a wonderful homecoming.

May 11, 1541.   Today was the first time I had alone with Gregory. How I lauded him for the final work on the volume which I had not seen until surprised by the package from Monsieur Etienne. How did he know that twenty copies would be exactly the number I needed for all of the members of the Confraternity?

"Why, in the note you left for me the day before you departed, Sister Angelica, you said twenty would be the correct number."

"What note, Gregory? I was too busy with the girls the night before and couldn't have…" But then my voice drifted off, and I said, simply, "I understand."

June 9, 1541.   The summer is passing quickly, and I am renewed once more here at the Orphanage. Eulogio has told wonderful tales of the inner magic that comes to his hands whenever he begins to carve. "Yes, it is something of a vision, but it is also combined with both an understanding and a compelling need. Although I enjoy carving the toys and furniture, when I carve the religious objects my hands are truly carving away all the surplus wood to simply reveal the images already existing within." I took his arm and thanked him warmly for his caring and sharing.

July 18, 1541.   I have given a great many lessons in the instruction room, and I listen once more in my heart to the fond memories the lessons bring to me. More than ever this summer I am enjoying working with all the girls. Each girl is a creation of beauty, and an important figure in God's plan.

August 10, 1541.   I have had letters from both Paris and Orléans telling of the successful work that the members of the Confraternity have been doing, teaching among the strife-bound families in each city. I will leave tomorrow to visit both groups.

September 19, 1541.   Once again we have completed the Forty Hours' Devotion in Orléans. We have had many more wishing to participate this year and spend their time watching and praying during the Devotion. Illness is ravaging the streets of this fair city.

December 18, 1541.   Yesterday I returned again to the Orphanage. Emily, Sister Zoraida, and the girls have continued to prepare many verses and designs for cards of greeting, to forward to Monsieur Estienne for publishing, in accordance with our agreement of six years ago. The Orphanage has benefited greatly from the arrangement.

December 25, 1541.   There was a light snowfall last evening, and the trees were sparkling and the ground was clean and white as we approached the Church for Christmas Mass. Sunlight streamed through the colored side windows with the images of the young Jesus. A golden wand of light pierced the circular window high above the Angel in Blue spreading luminosity across the Crib. The girls sang like angels—high, clear, beautiful voices. A shutter swept over the congregation as Father Leonard began his sermon: "What then does this Birth mean, this opening flower of infinite, eternal love? To us it means a divine redemption, an heirloom of graces; the beginning of unending companionship, a divine brotherhood and sisterhood, a pledge of eternal life. To Jesus, the Great Little One, it meant overflowing love, and what love always brings—sorrow, suffering, sacrifice."

Later, in the early evening, we celebrated the Procession of the Candles, and heard Father Leonard speak again: "What a beautiful sight the angels saw that Christmas! With guidance from the star and in wondering awe, the shepherds drew near to Mary's side, and kneeling by her, adored their Savior, Christ the Lord. All that was fairest upon earth was there. As the day advanced, other simple souls came flocking in from the fields and hamlets—not unlike you and me—and in silent rapture adored the newborn King. And just as His first day closed, let us now keep our minds fixed on this mystery wrought!"

Oh, the Spirit was with all of us tonight!

December 27, 1541.   All of us at the Orphanage enjoyed a great meal prepared by April, and we applauded her for it. A surprise tasty treat were loaves of sweet yellow bread, served with warm honey. The bread was made from meal ground from kernels, which had been removed from the "ears" (as the children called them), of the mahiz plants nurtured in the fields by Robert that summer, grown from the seeds presented by King Charles. It was a great Christmas party, and we sang songs until all of the littlest girls had fallen asleep. What a wonderful family God has given me!

1542

January 8, 1542.   It is time once again to return to the Convent and the first three days of the instruction period, where all the members must assemble to renew our commitment to the principles of the Confraternity. Mother Superior will assume all the duties of the instruction this year, and I shall travel to Orléans with the members assigned there to assist in furthering the missionary work.

January 17, 1542.   Orléans is bitter cold, and the illness is worse than last year. Many of our friends have died, but we will continue to work in the name of the Lord, celebrating his Divine Presence.

February 8, 1542.   One of our members has become very ill, and I am afraid for her. We obtained certain ointments from the apothecary, but the fever continues. We are spending all day in prayer.

February 11, 1542.   We have lost one of our members. She died near midnight. This is the saddest of days.

February 28, 1542.   Another member and I have both been ill, but today we are better. We entreated Saint Francis that we may continue with our work, and we recite together one of his favorite prayers:

Lord, make me an instrument of thy peace.
Where there is hatred, let me bring love;
Where there is injury, pardon.
Where there is doubt, faith;
Where there is despair, hope.
Where there is darkness, light;
Where there is sadness, joy;
And all for thy mercy's sake.
O Divine Master,
Grant that I may not so much seek to be consoled
As to console;
To be understood as to understand;
To be loved as to love.
For it is in giving that we receive;
It is in pardoning that we are pardoned;
And it is in dying that we are born to eternal life.

March 20, 1542.   We have struggled through a very cold winter, and we do not have the strength that we had formerly. Many of us have had bouts of illness. Our friends in Jesus have assisted us whenever they can, and we continue to share the love of the Divine Presence. We are bound together in His love and compassion.

March 28, 1542.   Last night I had strong visions of the family at the Orphanage, in their warm inner circle. In my mind I visited our Church of Saint Francis of Assisi, and saw sunbeams coming through Grandpapa's round stained glass window, and I sipped a cup of Grandmama's hot tea. Both Emily and Michael were by my side.

March 30, 1542.   This morning in my mind I saw little René, who first asked me, "Where do I find Jesus?" She gave me the strength I needed to see me through another day. I cannot despair, and I continue to hold Jesus close in my heart. The Angel in Blue looked down, and a breeze stirred her blue robes.

March 31, 1542. In my imagination, Emily held my hand today and fed me some warm broth. I was cold again, just like that December day when Mama had died. All the other sisters hovered around me, with serious looks on their faces.

April 2, 1542. Jesus spoke to me last night. He asked me if I wanted to follow Him and I answered that I was here to serve Him, and I would do whatever He ordered for me. The sisters were all about again, and I beseeched them not to weep and lament any more. Please remember me at the Lord's altar wherever you may go to teach.

April 3, 1542. Papa and I were in front of the Cathedral of Notre Dame in the fading sunlight and I counted all of the great stone arches this time as a group of ragged little orphan girls were peering at us from around a corner of the building while the organ grinder's little monkey was jumping up and down and up and down and up and down until a little girl came by and dropped a coin in his little hat and then the little girl turned around and looked at me and said I shouldn't cry because she knew of a peaceful Orphanage in the country that had geese and chickens and dogs and kittens that I could play with and she thought I could live there and sing sweet songs with a beautiful person called Sister Angelica who would show me how to find Jesus.

Mourning Angel, metal casting found in an old cemetery

Epilogue by Mother Superior

April 3, 1542.   Early this morning, before the lessons began, I sat in the library contemplating our labor of love in our Confraternity, and the impact of Sister Angelica on my life and the energy she has brought to the Convent. I recalled the first morning when she arrived, nearly twenty years ago. Such a little girl she was, just bursting with enthusiasm. I thought of the drive she had to serve our Lord and do His will. I thought of the knowledge she brought in her ability to read and write. And I thought of the first books she brought to the Convent, and how careful we had to be then that the books were all proper.

My thoughts were drifting in and out as the early sunlight streamed through the window, when slowly I detected a presence unlike anything else I had ever experienced. There seemed to be a faint blue mist in front of the largest bookcase. And then … and then her face appeared. Sister Angelica! "What?" I questioned, nearly aloud. Had I lapsed into complete reverie? Sister Angelica's full body then appeared, in her deep maroon habit.

"Sister Angelica, is that you? Are you not in Orléans? Why didn't you notify us you were returning?" But it was she, and yet it wasn't she. She gazed strangely forward.

"I have left you, Mother Superior," she whispered. "I am no longer as you once knew me. I have found Jesus and He is real. But do not weep, for I am not asleep. I ride on the sunlight beam and within the passing cloud. Please inform all my dear friends that I shall forever watch over the Confraternity. Continue to live in the message of God, and spread the word of the Divine Presence."

I reached out to touch her, but then the vision disappeared. I felt faint, for I knew Sister Angelica had been here.

 # Epilogue by Emily

April 3, 1542.   The sky was especially bright this morning before dawn. I had arisen early to help April with the daily preparations. As the sun peeked over the horizon, René, who always liked to be by my side, and I, walked down the path to the Church to say our morning prayers together. It was quite cool, and we pulled our shawls around us.

After a few moments sitting in quiet prayer, my thoughts began to wander. My eyes traveled from the round stained glass window, just catching the early sunbeams, down across the altar and the relic of Saint Francis of Assisi and up to the Angel in Blue. I blinked. Was there a breeze in the Church? I thought I saw a ripple in the angel's robe. "But that couldn't be," I thought, "the robe is carved from wood. But there it is again, a quivering in the robe." I touched René's arm. "Look," I whispered, "the robe!" I could tell in her eyes that she saw it too.

And then, out of a blue mist, faint at first, then more defined, appeared Sister Angelica. "Is that you Sister Angelica?" gasped René. We were frozen in half fear, half elation.

"Yes, I am here," Sister Angelica said quietly. "But I have left you and I am now with Jesus. I have found Jesus. Be glad for me, and do not weep. I am the rainbow in the dark sky. I am the chirp of the nesting bluebirds. Please inform all my dear family that I shall forever watch over the Orphanage."

She faded away into the soft mist, and then it, too, disappeared. René and I sat holding on to one another. "Let us bring the family and a few of the older girls here, to tell them we saw," I finally said.

"And Michael! Let us summon Michael to travel to Orléans quickly, to confirm what might have befallen Sister Angelica," said René.

April 7, 1542. It has been a very sad four days, with no further news. But about noon, down the road, appeared Michael and a wagon bearing a shrouded body. It was true as we had been told—as Sister Angelica herself had told us.

"Let us have her rest here in the Church for one day," said Michael at last through the tears. "Then we shall have a final Mass, and sing and praise her wonderful life, and lay her to rest near the orchard."

We mourned and prayed, each in our own way each according to our own needs. The girls slipped silently in and out of the Church, not believing it could be true— that they would never see Sister Angelica again.

April 8, 1542. At noon the bells tolled. They tolled and tolled and tolled, for Gregory could not let go of the rope in his grief. The Church was overflowing into the aisles with all the neighbors from the villages who had so loved Sister Angelica. The girls were in front, along with the sisters who had arrived, each comforting one another. The Mass said by Father Leonard was solemn. The girls sang beautiful music that they had been practicing. This was new choral music recently sent up by Monsieur Estienne, who had just received it from Rome. It was written by a new composer, appointed to Saint Peter's by Pope Paul III, whose name is Pierliugi da Palestrina.

Father Leonard was quite emotional as he began his final prayer. "This morning, as I began dressing for this Mass, a piece of paper fell from inside the sleeve of my alb. I do not know how it got there. Let me read it to you, slowly, in memory of Sister Angelica:

> 'Do not mourn,
> But rejoice in the lighting of a new star in the heavens;
> Look beyond earth's shadows, pray to trust our Father's will.
> Do not grieve my memory and weep,
> For I love you dearly still, I do not sleep.
> I am a thousand winds that blow;
> I am the diamond glints on snow;
> I am the sunlight on ripened grain,
> I am the gentle springtime rain.
> I am the strength of the surging sea,
> I am the dew kissed ginger in the valley.
> When you awaken in the morning hush,
> I am the swift uplifting rush
> Of quiet birds in circled flight.
> I am the soft star that shines at night.
> Do not stand at my grave and cry.
> I am not there; I did not die.' "

And once again I thought I saw, out of the corner of my eye a ripple float across the robe of the Angel in Blue.

Epilogue from the New World

On the day of Sister Angelica's death, a grand windstorm swept across a small range of mountains on the west coast of the continent which was later to be called North America. Little was known in Europe about this new land, for the Europeans had first set foot on its easterly shores only 50 years earlier. The Spanish were busy with their obsession of finding the Seven Cities of Gold in what is now New Mexico. It would be another six months before Cabrillo would discover San Diego Bay, and perhaps one hundred and fifty years before any European explorer would view the mountains now being swept by the grand windstorm.

The unlikely names of "cedars", "ponderosas", and "sugar pines" would much later be attached to the tall swaying conifers. The trees were nestled along a narrow granite mountain ridge at an elevation of 5600 feet. They provided cool summer shade for the deer, bear and Serrano Indians that inhabited the area.

A two-year-old cedar tree

The grand windstorm swept the cedar trees clear of their seed pods. The pods swirled all about, covering the forest floor. One of the seed kernels from a pod found firm shelter tucked behind a small rock next to a lingering patch of snow, safe from the ever-searching blue jays and squirrels. It was a drier summer than usual—all summers were without rain—but when the autumn rains came, the seed quickly sprouted, and in the second year took on the leafy characteristics of a tiny cedar tree. Already the greenery gave off the pungent odor of incense cedar.

During its younger years the cedar tree bent so that its tip touched the ground under the heavy weight of wet snow. But after the winter seasons it straightened again, raising its red-brown branches to the sky. The tree thrived in its ideal setting. It gave high shelter to the jays and squirrels, protecting them from the marauding summer ravens. Upward and upward it grew, becoming a landmark called Cedar Giant to the Indians who explored this area for acorns and small game.

Cedar Giant reached maturity on the moderate west-facing slope. It was 100 feet from a small stream which drained the melting snows to the creek below. Its roots reached out to tap this continual moisture. The tree lived far beyond maturity, and bore the scars of forest fires, set by summer lightning, that occasionally thundered through the area. It grew additional bark to cover its scars. And so it lived on into the mid-Nineteenth Century.

Pioneers came into the valleys and foothills surrounding this narrow mountain range in 1852. As their settlements grew, so did their need for lumber for their structures and wood for their fuel. By 1870 they had blazed an oxen trail up the steep mountain and set up lumber mills in the dense forest areas. In 1875 the Tyler Brothers, looking for more trees for their mill along Grass Valley Creek, walked up the slope and spotted Cedar Giant. Its size and maturity astonished them. It represented thousands of cedar roofing shakes and decay-resistant lumber for house footings.

In the winter of 1875–76, Cedar Giant was felled. The first wedge-cut was placed on the west, down-slope side, penetrating a full 14 inches. Then the two-man saw began its final cut on the east side, only two feet about the ground. It took more than two hours to complete the final cut—a cut through 300 years of history—a cut back into time to the era of Sister Angelica and Emily and Michael and the Orphanage of Meaux.

The stump of Cedar Giant remains to this day. It is located on Lot 271 of Tract 7201, just above Grizzly Road. The burn marks are still there; the saw blade cuts are still visible. Every year the squirrels peel off a few more shreds of the red-brown bark to line their nests. Every year pine needles from surrounding new cedars, ponderosas and sugar pines cover its top.

The stump of Cedar Giant will survive perhaps another 100 years or even more, well through the twenty-first century—long enough to celebrate the 500th anniversary of the life of Saint Sister Angelica.

The End